PARENTING:
A Journey of Faith While Navigating the Detours

Finding Strength From Pain And Creating an Atmosphere of Steadfast Love.

LUCY WATANI-SIMIYU

Copyright © 2021 Lucy Watani-Simiyu.

All rights reserved. No part of this book may be used or reproduced by any means, graphic, electronic, or mechanical, including photocopying, recording, taping or by any information storage retrieval system without the written permission of the author except in the case of brief quotations embodied in critical articles and reviews.

This book is a work of non-fiction. Unless otherwise noted, the author and the publisher make no explicit guarantees as to the accuracy of the information contained in this book and in some cases, names of people and places have been altered to protect their privacy.

WestBow Press books may be ordered through booksellers or by contacting:

WestBow Press
A Division of Thomas Nelson & Zondervan
1663 Liberty Drive
Bloomington, IN 47403
www.westbowpress.com
844-714-3454

Because of the dynamic nature of the Internet, any web addresses or links contained in this book may have changed since publication and may no longer be valid. The views expressed in this work are solely those of the author and do not necessarily reflect the views of the publisher, and the publisher hereby disclaims any responsibility for them.

Any people depicted in stock imagery provided by Getty Images are models, and such images are being used for illustrative purposes only. Certain stock imagery © Getty Images.

Unless marked otherwise, all Scripture quotations are taken from The Holy Bible, English Standard Version® (ESV®), Copyright © 2001 by Crossway, a publishing ministry of Good News Publishers. All rights reserved.

Scripture quotations marked NIV are taken from The Holy Bible, New International Version®, NIV® Copyright © 1973, 1978, 1984, 2011 by Biblica, Inc.® Used by permission. All rights reserved worldwide.

ISBN: 978-1-6642-4066-7 (sc)
ISBN: 978-1-6642-4068-1 (hc)
ISBN: 978-1-6642-4067-4 (e)

Library of Congress Control Number: 2021914468

Print information available on the last page.

WestBow Press rev. date: 07/28/2021

I give all the glory to our Almighty God for his great faithfulness and mercy and for making my dream a reality. When all hope seemed lost after sickness with COVID-19, in the midst of writing my manuscript, he miraculously healed and restored me. I give him all the glory and adoration. "And I thank him who has given me strength, Christ Jesus our Lord, because he judged me faithful, appointing me to his service" (1 Timothy 1:12).

This book is dedicated to my late parents, Lydiah Nyambura Watani and Jeremiah Watani Ngatia, for their tireless dedication and love. They helped me and my siblings grow to fulfill God's purpose. I am eternally grateful!

My most profound appreciation goes to my dear husband, Bob, for his encouragement of and inspiration for this book's research and editing. He enabled me to reach my God-given potential as I wrote this book. Above all, he is an invaluable partner in this experience of parenting our three loving sons and adorable daughter. He is a man of a few words loaded with wisdom, and his insights and suggestions were invaluable in preparing the final manuscript. I am honored to call this humble man my sweetheart.

I dedicate this book to my Loving children, Kevin, Derrick, Roy, and Angel. Your love and support are priceless! This book would not have been possible without your uniqueness and the precious gifts you are to me. I am eternally grateful and love you.

I also dedicate this book to my real blood sisters, "sisters of Grace" Wanjiku and Margaret. I fondly refer to them as my big sisters. We have intimately shared true sisterly love and fellowship through the highs and lows of our parenting journeys. Your iron has sharpened my iron, and I believe mine has sharpened yours too. Thank you for bearing my burdens, and above all, thank you for your daily prayers and encouragement when I was sick with COVID-19. What the enemy meant for evil, the Lord has turned it for my good to complete this book for his glory. I love and appreciate you.

To Praying Moms: Thank you for intimately sharing your

sisterly love. You are a model of true sisterhood. Above all, thank you for continually praying for our children and families. There is no better hood than sisterhood! God bless.

To my faith family at Bearcreek Church. Special thanks to Pastor David Welch for faithfully preaching God's word and bringing transformation in our lives! Sister B.J Welch your intercessory and teaching of the undiluted word is forever ingrained in my heart!I love and appreciate you! To Linda Gaskins, Carol Landry, and ladies in the Bible study class your iron sharpens mine and thank you for your fellowship and friendship.My sisters Candy McLaughlin, Gail Garner,Sheri Campbell, your love and support over the years is much appreciated. Special thanks to the youth ministry for walking alongside our children and helping them find their true identity in Christ. I am eternally grateful.

To Pastor Zeek Avelar, youth pastor, and Drea Avelar: thanks for introducing Jesus to our children in a way that compelled them and many other children to follow him and love God's Word. Special thanks for giving our children opportunities to be servant leaders, carrying the mantle on to college and in life. I couldn't be more proud and grateful.

To the Katy Lakewood fellowship: God directs our paths in life regarding the places we go and live. In many ways our lives are changed by very special neighbors. Great value is the servant leadership of Brother Tunde Afinni, Sister Stella Afinni, Brother Ayoola Ekisola, and Sister Toyin Ekisola. May the Lord continue to bless you as you minister to families and share and model the true love of Christ. I appreciate you!

To "Shiprahs and Puahs Sisters" in Houston: you are my sisters in Christ and prayerful and caring ladies. Thank you for being steadfast in praying for children and families and for standing in the gap. Special thanks to Chaplain Tabitha Gachiengo: you are an epitome of a great mother, wife, and servant leader, inspiring parents to take the Word of God seriously and apply it to transform lives in families and communities.

I am also grateful to the pastors and able ministers and friends in our communities who nourish our spirits, care for ours souls, and dedicate their lives to serve between the troubled waters of our parental and familial experiences with the solid reality of the gospel. I pray for the strength of your souls and abundance of life found in Jesus Christ.

> On the day I called, you answered me; my strength of soul you increased. (Psalm 138:3)

Praise for *Parenting: A Journey of Faith While Navigating The Detours*

Finding Strength From Pain And Creating an Atmosphere of Steadfast Love.

Lucy Simiyu is the personification of God's wisdom in parenting. For as long as I've known her, Lucy has earnestly sought to understand and exemplify the beautiful responsibility all parents have in reflecting the character and nature of who God is to her children. By grace, her efforts have produced much fruit. It is abundantly clear that Lucy's perspective and approach to parenting derives from the incredible wealth of knowledge given to us in the Word of God. Her faithful application of these truths are more than evident in lives of her children. They indeed "rise and call her blessed." Each of them has matured into people-loving, God-fearing leaders of leaders. As a youth pastor, being witness to this firsthand has been one of the chief blessings of my ten-plus years in family ministry. This book is a valuable book for every parent!

Pastor Zeek Avelar
Youth Pastor, Houston Tx

For the majority of us, the parenting journey is an adventure laden with many mixed blessings. Many times we grope in the dark, too afraid of any light, fearing that it may illuminate our failures, but hoping to arrive at some destination all right. Lucy is a deeply spiritual, professional, practical, and intentional parent who openly and lovingly journeys with her children at their different levels. Her honesty and willingness to give us a glimpse into her parenting journey has been a great privilege. Lucy has helped me appreciate every parenting moment, warts and all. I know that I am never alone, and in the end, God always swings it in the balance of victory!

In this book, Lucy confronts parental challenges with a Godly perspective and practical application. Prepare to be challenged, equipped, and blessed by Lucy!

Dr. Lucy Kanya
Assistant Professor, LSE
London

The speed of technological development today has put a strain on parenting. The generation gap is widening as the world gets faster than the pace of parenting. As a chaplain working in the church with preteens, I know that parents have expressed a need to learn how to parent in this day and age. In this book, Lucy, a Christian counselor, wife, and mother, has combined practical and theological parenting skills, making her book a must-have for any parent.

Chaplain Tabitha Gachiengu
BSN, BA-Psychology, CPE
Houston Tx

Lucy has the God-fearing heart every caring Christian mother should cultivate. When I have been blessed to see Lucy lovingly relate to her kids, her patient ways of sharing Scripture-based wisdom are always a shining testimony. I thank the Lord for leading Lucy to compile the parenting wisdom he has given her into a book. I feel certain the Lord will richly bless you through the valuable wisdom Lucy has learned to embrace. Highest praises to our sovereign God for how Lucy prayerfully relies on him and his Word of unchanging truth, whatever trials he may allow to come her way.

Beaj Welch
Servant Leader
Houston

I have known Lucy Simiyu for over twenty years and am familiar with her passion in building a strong family. I am happy that she has decided to develop a guide for parenting, and I cannot recommend this book highly enough. It is both theological and practical—a rare combination of a parenting book. Lucy shows you a bigger picture of Christ in your parenting journey and walking by grace through faith.

Evangelist Isaac Kariuki
CEO and Founder, **diasporamessenger.com**
Silver Springs, MD

Sister Lucy is a Godly woman who exhibits traits of virtuous living both in her personal and business life. She is a loving wife and mother with a pure heart dedicated to raising good and healthy homes in our communities. This is an incredibly significant book for parenting. Read it today!

Ayo Ekisola
Leader, **Katy Lakewood Fellowship**
Houston

I have been blessed over the years to watch Lucy and her husband raise their four dynamic children. Their deep and consistent dependence on God and His Word has been a beautiful testimony of God's faithfulness in their lives. Her book is a welcome tool for parents at all stages. It provides a biblical, practical, and well-balanced approach to parenting for our times.

June Onguko-Matindu
Realtor
Houston

Lucy is a loving and dedicated mother who prays for not only her children but also other children. Lucy started a praying group of mothers called Momma and Dotta. The group prays and shares parenting experiences. Lucy is also a member of

Praying Moms, a group that meets twice a week for Bible study and prays for children. She is a loving mother, and you can tell by how free she is with her children. Your heart will soar as your read this book. Despite enduring parental pain, detours in your parenting journey, or shattered faith, you are reminded of anchor-type, weighty, real hope in Jesus.

Talya King
Pastor, Far Above Rubies Ministry
Houston

This book challenges, rejuvenates, and renews your parental journey. It contains Godly revelations and reflections for raising children who stay grounded in Christian principles. For more parental insights, read this book today.

Emily Soroko
Author, *Rising Above Adversity*
Fairfax, VA

Lucy is a friend and a leader who wears many hats. She is a nurse, a public health educator, a biblical counselor, a wife, and a mother. She is a leader in our community, and I have worked with Lucy on many platforms. She educates and inspires our community to be physically, mentally, socially, and spiritually healthy. Lucy knows that the foundation of a strong and successful society is the family unit. She is a passionate educator in this area, and she does it by example as a wife and a mother. You will be inspired by this book, and together we can change the world one family at a time.

Alice Munyua
Family Nurse Practitioner, Author, and Radio Host
North Carolina

At a time when parenting is facing incredible challenges, Lucy's book is a very timely gift to humanity. I am praying that it will soon be accessible to as many parents as soon possible to bring intervention where necessary.

I have known and ministered with Lucy for a couple of years. I have found a great friend and sister in the Lord who takes faith and matters of God seriously in every aspect of her life. As is common to women who also reflect on motherhood, Lucy invited me into the group *Praying Moms* to pray for one of the children in crisis. That child is now healed and restored to health! In my interaction with Lucy, I have found Lucy as one who considers parenting a sacred calling to be taken seriously. Lucy also shared with us the need to openly communicate with our children in a way that will build their trust in us and help them call on us in their times of need. Lucy believes in disciplining and coaching our children in a loving way, even while taking necessary disciplinary action to help mould their lives. As for her parenting, I have known Lucy to have God and spirituality be the foundation of everything she does in and for her family. Lucy is one invaluable, well-rounded parenting role model at a time when parents are challenged in every way and need Godly guidance, motivation, and encouragement. This is who Lucy is to our generation: a gift and a role model.

Read this book. The compelling stories and life-changing revelations will challenge you to live up to your ambassadorial call as a parent.

Rev. Dr. Penny Njoroge,
Author, Clinical Psychologist, and Drug
and Substance Abuse Therapist
Alabama

A godly mother is a gift to her children because she prays for and over them, encourages them, loves them, and instills good values. A godly mother is also one who is willing to let her children walk their own paths as she mentors, coaches, and prayerfully encourages them. Lucy embodies all these qualities.

I have watched her interact with her children as their greatest cheerleader, celebrating them at every turn. Lucy is a godly mother who embodies love, grace, wisdom, and a prayerful spirit. This book is a hallmark for parental teaching. Read it!

Dr. Pauline Akatsa-Hinga
CEO and Founder, Brokenly Flawless
Houston Tx.

This is such a timely book. Lucy, my dear sister-in-Christ, has written this book for all parents. And especially for parents who find themselves in a stormy season. As parents facing the hard realities of a child whose life has taken a detour, our hope is in God and his Word and his faithfulness. Lucy has so much love for family. And as she points out, we are imperfect parents with a perfect God. She points to the promises of God and through this book offers so much encouragement from the Word of God.

Carol Landry
Servant Leader BCC
Houston Tx.

Contents

Acknowledgments xvii
Foreword xix
Preface xxi
Introduction xxv

Chapter 1   Seasons In Parenting When Nothing
            Makes Sense 1
Chapter 2   Detours 19
Chapter 3   God Makes Sense 33
Chapter 4   Stand Out In Fit-In Generation 59
Chapter 5   Grace Abounds 89
Chapter 6   GPS Signal Lost, Navigation Rerouting 115
Chapter 7   From Faith To Faith 126
Chapter 8   We Do Not Know What to Do, but Our
            Eyes Are on You 144
Chapter 9   Pray For Me, I am A Parent 155
Chapter 10 The DNA of God's Steadfast Love 188
Chapter 11 Becoming Perfectly Imperfect 196
Chapter 12 Beyond The Detour 211

Bibliographical References 221
About the Author 223

Acknowledgments

I appreciate my loving son Kevin for his encouragement—and most importantly his computer expertise in easing my burden of reviewing and editing the final manuscript. Your stories, experiences, and suggestions spiced up the stories in this book. Son, you are a testament of God's love: incredible, unfailing, and infinite. You are special, and I love you, Kevo!

I wish to thank my amazing son Derrick, for his assistance after I became ill with COVID-19 and found myself mentally and emotionally exhausted. He helped with finishing the manuscript, though I found purpose in my pain. Thank you, son, for challenging me to review this book based on your feedback from your Christian leadership training, and for taking the time to fill in the appropriate illustrations and transitions. You were God-sent at a time I needed a helping hand. I pray the time you took to work on your mother's manuscript will always be one of the most memorable times we shared. I will forever treasure this book because it was written with the help of my son. I love you, Kiki.

To my amazing son Roy: Your motivation and encouragement and moral support even in your final year of college is much appreciated. It warms my heart to see you and your siblings following in the footsteps of Christ. I may have taught you how, but you have proven the reason for giving you wings and helping me fly! I am proud of you, and I love you, son.

To my adorable daughter, Angel. You took the time and effort to write the Bible verses in ESV. May God's word forever be hidden in your heart. Thank you for your patience and kindness. I love you, my Monaji!

Thank you, my loving sister Margaret Watani-Waithaka, for your assistance in reviewing this book and writing the foreword. Margaret, you are not only my big sister but are also a jewel in God's kingdom who has taught me profound truth in speech with a deep revelation of the knowledge of God. You bring out my God-given potential. I love you, big sis!

Carrie Poffenberger: Thank you, my dear friend, for writing the killer introduction and the insights on the exegesis of Scripture. I am humbled! Though it has been many years since we took biblical counseling classes, you are God's perfect choice for truth for parents while creating an option to easily personalize the principles in this book and share it with other hurting parents.

I am writing this book with a parent and child in mind: for that child whose life has taken a detour, and for a parent in pain facing hard realities while navigating detours. I pray that God will use my efforts to strengthen you and repair your shattered faith in your journey. The Lord is near, and he loves you. So do I.

Foreword

When Lucy asked me to write a foreword for this book, I was excited and humbled not because she is my younger sister (I like to call her Lil Sister), but because I knew that she had written on a topic about which she is passionate and experienced.

Lucy is a compelling narrator, and in this book, I saw her own parenting journeys and biblical counseling skills beautifully intersect. She takes the reader through the highs of hopes and dreams that all parents have for their children, as well as to the sometimes crushing reality of broken dreams, bad choices, and dark places along the journey, where it seems like all hope is lost. Some of the tough questions we face as parents are asked and answered in this book. For example, What do I do when my child makes the wrong choices? How do I deal with contrary or counterculture? What about parenting guilt? Where is God in all this?

Thankfully, Lucy does not leave the reader in the valley of despair. She is quick to point the reader to where hope lies: in the faithfulness of God. I am also excited that alongside this book are study tools and resources that will help both individuals and small-group studies.

I pray that this book will be a tool in your hands to transform your own parenting journey and instill hope in the faithfulness of God. It is a must-have resource for every parent, irrespective of one's stage of parenting.

Margaret Waithaka
President, Praying Moms Ministries International, Baltimore

Preface

Lucy and I met at Bible college in the middle of Houston, Texas. Every week for several years, we shared a table and sat across from one another. As a caregiver at the time to my daughter, I was taken by Lucy's choice to be a hospice nurse. There is not a whole lot of people of whom you can ask, "Have you held the dying?" She has. I have too. It is one of the most humbling experiences you can have. Likewise, ministering to the people they leave behind can be equally humbling. We both started biblical counseling to be able to minister to others. As life would have it, God was teaching us for, well, us.

We would both need the truth of God like our lungs need air. Sometimes in the darkest of night, the only flicker of light is the truth of God's Word. If you do not know it, then you have nothing to hold to when you find yourself there.

My firstborn son, Jeremiah, and my daughter, Lily, were born with a genetic disorder that caused epilepsy and severe neurological problems. My children sometimes had hundreds of seizures per day, as well as sleeping and eating issues, and they required much care. It was a privilege to be their mom. While they were with us, they suffered physically, yet God never left them or forsook them. Jeremiah lived to be three and a half years old. He passed away in the night from a seizure, but I know the Lord called him home. Lily lived to be nine years old, and while her body failed her, God was faithful to her.

I do not say these things to comfort myself, although they do comfort me. I tell them because I experienced the grace and goodness of God amid my children's suffering. I say them because they are the truth of God's Word, which does not change. I prayed and believed for healing, and the Lord chose to give them the ultimate healing. That healing will never be taken away. The wind and waves of pain and suffering for them were met with the Lord's comfort: "It is finished" (John 19:30). Moreover, they live in the light of his glory. I still ache at times to see, smell, and touch them again, but I know one day I will. I grieve with hope.

There are places in the Lord, depths in him, and depths in me that I would not have touched without hardship. I now have the privilege of hindsight to look back on those horrible, tragic moments and long to be as near to God as the brokenness of heartbreak brings you. That may sound foolish or weird, but it is true.

Parents, there is always grace available. Always. It flows from his throne like love, justice, holiness, and mercy. Grace is not just unmerited favor. It is power. Grace picks you up and moves you forward wherever you find yourself. Grace sometimes comes through the kind words of a friend who get you through the challenging moment you are in. Alternatively, at the end of a long, hard day of parenting, you may want to give up, but your child gives you the biggest hug. Sometimes it's only supernatural how you get through, but you did it by God's grace. You may not have the grace you need for tomorrow, but if you allow yourself to see it, you will find the grace you need for the moment you are in. Leave tomorrow for tomorrow.

I write from a healing and hindsight perspective, but Lucy walks you through the raw, ugly moments that come when the tragedy first strikes. She doesn't shy away from some tragedies that become long, cold treks up Mount Everest. She allows you to not be a hero or an unobtainable version of someone's faithful Christian highlight reel. You can be right where you are, yet hopeful. The truth she shares brings you some freedom during the parenting struggle. She gives direction and guidance without shame.

Lucy holds several undergraduate degrees and a master's

degree. She speaks several different languages, which she uses to approach this subject matter holistically. She is one of the warmest, God-loving women I have ever met. She is a warrior queen who knows how to battle and intercede. It is a gift of the Holy Spirit. Her book reflects her faith and shares wisdom for intercession. Parents, if you find yourself in a challenging season, please read this book and drink deeply from the truth she shares from God's Word and comfort from her vulnerability.

My prayer for you parents who find yourselves reading this book is that you seek and find God, that his comfort wraps around you, and that you grow and mature in Christ through the painful parts of parenting. May God be closer than a friend, and may you touch new depths in him. Amen.

Carrie Poffenberger
Prayer Minister
Bellville, Texas

Introduction

Thank you for your interest in this journey to become a grace-based parent. Our best efforts sometimes fail us as we watch our children take a detour from our expectations and God's Word. I am not the author and finisher of my faith story. I would never have had the courage to write my parenting story and other parents' experiences with the twists and turns it has taken. I have walked through seasons of devastation beyond what I thought I could survive. But I have also been incredibly blessed and humbled because God has proven himself faithful beyond my ability to comprehend.

The motivation for writing this book emanates from my experiences as a mother and from the encounters of fellow parents and believers in the Lord Jesus Christ who have many unanswered questions on the parenting journey. My inspiration for writing also came out of a realization of big-picture parenting. It came after a season when nothing made sense and it felt like God was abandoning me. It was a time filled with anxiety and heartbreak, and with many questions unanswered.

In my parental journey and counselling sessions, the experiential learning from thousands of parents raised many questions. I journaled them over several years, not sure of the direction, but as David in the Psalms delighted in the Lord, I obeyed to write this book. I tell my story to bring him glory! Can children abandon their values? Can children question their faith in God in a nerve-wracking way to parents and yet continue to function sanely? There were times in my parenting journey where I felt like a failure. I was embarrassed to ask for prayers or support from the body of Christ. I blamed myself. Where did I go wrong? What seemed to be a simple verse became complicated. Proverbs 22:6 states, "Train up a child in the way he should go; even when he is old, he will not depart from it."

I needed a practical reality in parenting, not to undermine or take lightly the pain of seeing a child stray from faith. When falling away from grace in my parental journey, I was put in a place of surrender. I searched for answers. The healing came in the realization of my purpose, role, and calling as a parent. Christ's death, burial, and resurrection make us brand-new. Forgiveness and turning to the Lord lets his Holy Spirit lead and guide us. I had an understanding of my relationship with God and my children. There was a calling to parents with a loving heart, joy, and grace. Faith in God is at the heart of what I am and what I do as a wife, parent, and friend in my day-to-day life!

I carry the hope we have in Christ to other parents. My parenting journey is not an end in itself; as Apostle Paul says in 2 Corinthians 4:5, "For what we proclaim is not ourselves, but Jesus Christ as Lord, with ourselves as your servants for Jesus' sake." This book is also for our children, who have so many experiences that do not make sense and the lessons learned from the anticipated perfect parental trip. The journey is not without yield signs, bumps, detours, pauses, and stop signs. This book points you to the source of joy in your journey by pointing you to God's Word, the truth that sets you free when the journey gets weary. The blueprint still works—not to make you guilty but to liberate you.

Do I like the experience? Absolutely, and I cannot quit. I guess you may have a similar version of my journey. Parents' best efforts sometimes fail them as they watch their children take a detour from their expectations, training, and teaching. The environment and cultural conflicts all too often play a part in children's molding. Unfortunately, we cannot control the outcomes and have to watch the consequences of choices with a roller coaster of emotions.

It is challenging when our parenting journey looks nothing like we expected. What is an expected event turns out to be a process. However, instead of tying our hope to specific outcomes, let us connect ourselves to the very heart of God. You as a parent may not be able to see it right now, but the story God is writing for our children and us is ultimately so much better than anything we could write ourselves. Maybe you have been praying and reasoning with God. Hannah's release of Samuel reveals the attitude all Godly parents should adopt: "O LORD of hosts, if You will indeed look on the affliction of Your maidservant and remember me, and not forget Your maidservant, but will give Your maidservant a son, then I will give him to the LORD all the days of his life" (1 Samuel 1:11).

Nevertheless, though you know the Scripture lays out clear principles, all you can think is you dedicated your child to the Lord and taught him so that when he grows, he will not depart from it. And you know sons and daughters are like arrows to be aimed—and then released, as the psalmist states: "Like arrows in the hand of a warrior are children of one's youth" (Psalm 127:4). You say, "My children are not mine to keep, but mine to develop for God's glory." However, in my sight, it is pain, tears, restlessness, anger, and bitterness that do not make sense. It is too hard to bear to watch a child's detour from your expectations, to live with this disability on a child and detour from the truth of God's Word and upbringing. Maybe you are double-minded to continue serving God and continue with the fellowship in a troublesome circumstance.

Whatever situation you are in, God has a message for you as a parent. In the process, let us equip ourselves with the truth of God's Word to keep us sane and fulfill our ambassadorial calling. Apostle Paul stated in the book of Corinthians, "No temptation has overtaken you that is not common to man. God is faithful, and he will not let you be tempted beyond your ability, but with the temptation, he will also provide the way of escape, that you may be able to endure it" (1 Corinthians 10:13).

Maybe you are a parent who is paralyzed by fear of your

child's choices. You may be anxious, hopeless, and helpless about your child's future. Perhaps you are weighed down by guilt and shame, caught in a slump, overwhelmed with regret trapped in a dead-end parenting, and numb from a child's choice. You may be drowning in disappointment, anger, shame, and disappoint, unfilled spiritually so that God and his promises do not make sense.

With compelling storytelling and sound scriptural backup, this book gives you the biblical pathway to help you as a parent move beyond the pain of the present to a hope-filled future. Satan would love to rob you from realizing your God-powered potential and fulfilling your parenting role.

As the evil one presents obstacles to discourage you, God provides ways for you as a parent to be loosed from the chains holding you back—yes, that pain in parenting, a perspective on what it means to grow through tough parenting seasons.

If you want to rise from your circumstance, face the future with fearlessness, prevail over your present or past, live out your parental calling, or simply find purpose and joy in your parental stormy season to the best version God intended, then *Parenting: A Journey of Faith While Navigating the Detours* is for you. A rerouting handbook for the 21st Century Parent when the GPS signal is lost. This book helps you, as a parent, avoid the storm barrier and the sense that God is abandoning you and your children amid the storms of parenting.

I sought to give parents more than a theoretical knowledge of God. I wish to point parents toward yielding to a personal relationship in building, working in their parental journey according to his biblical precepts of unconditional love and immeasurable grace.

Everything that parents need to thrive in the twenty-first century—family matters, marriage, children, and parenting journey—have been lifelong priorities for me.

Based on my extensive study of both the Old and New Testaments and training as a biblical counsellor at a college of biblical studies, I have drawn together those timeless insights for building close and rewarding parenting journeys and strengthening family ties. By following a biblical exploration of God's purpose and plans for parents, parents realize their call as parents and as an essential part of God's mission to love and rescue the gift of children given to them. As the psalmist states, "Children are a gift from the LORD; they are a reward from him" (Psalm 127:3).

As a parent, you are well equipped and able to grow strong parenting skills despite the challenges, creating healthy children and a strong family. I take a clear-eyed look at those areas where parents and children often experience difficulties from their journey and experiences. These discussions are frank and direct and leave the parent filled with hope and encouragement.

My book is convenient for parents struggling with trials and heartaches they cannot understand, such as the following.

- Sudden death of a child from suicide
- Drug and alcohol addictions
- Teen pregnancy
- The prodigal child
- COVID-19 and other disease deaths
- Homelessness
- Different sexual orientations
- Depression
- Immorality
- Rebelliousness.

This book deals unflinchingly with when parents battle the troubling questions. The mind-boggling *why* is a journey of faith answered with the transforming power of the gospel, as stated in Hebrews 11:1, "Now Faith is the substance of things hoped for, the evidence of things not seen."

The journey in this book is not another ten or so steps to unlocking perfect parenting. Instead, it's an in-depth book of God's relationship with you as a parent and your child through the lens of the truth of his Word.

1

Seasons In Parenting When Nothing Makes Sense

> One characteristic that appears to be uniquely true of human beings is that we are meaning-seeking creatures.
> —Anonymous

One of the best seasons of my life has been getting to map out a thirty-two-hour family road trip to Canada. Getting behind the wheel for the first eight hours and looking forward to reaching the destination, despite the cost, was exciting. Google Maps gave great detail as the journey unwound. It was not without long hours containing dry spells, gas tank refueling experiences, a child at the back excited at every favorite food store, and the repeated anxious question of, "Are we there yet?" The answers were of assurance despite the many encounters of yields, exits, and sometimes detours as the GPS occasionally stated, "Now rerouting." The answers may not have made sense to a child focused on reaching the destination. The three other children, buckled in with seat belts, were chewing gum, snoozing, or playing games. Their loud giggles were an indication of a smooth, fun ride, and they were ready for a show-and-tell session at school. They trusted us, Mom and Daddy, to steer the wheel. The journey ended with lasting and beautiful memories despite delays and detours.

What does this mean to a parent with a well-planned journey for a child? The once bouncing baby's life has taken away the peace and laughter, and a parent asks, "God, when will this pain end? Am I there yet? Why did a loving God allow this to happen?" No theory or theology can satisfactorily explain these dilemmas posed by some fate and misfortune. As parents, we typically have plans for our children, and from the first cry to the time we anticipate to hit the exit button at eighteen years of age. But is it an exit?

Nevertheless, this is simply a mental map until the hard realities hit with delays, detours, and unexpected exits.

As the example I gave illustrates, the parental journey is a process, not a destination. There are many memories made despite the unexpected storms and challenges.

Who started your parental journey? Can you trust Him? He who started the journey will steer the wheel, so buckle up!

Have you ever watched a movie and asked, "Why did it have to end like that?" I am not a movie fan and find it hard to stay awake, even with buttered popcorn. I once watched a movie with my hubby, and we were was so depressed when it ended. It was an emotional roller coaster that battered our feelings and brought us almost to tears. There wasn't a dry eye in our living room. I wished I could rewrite the movie with my own ending, which would be happy and uplifting. Do you sometimes wish you could rewrite the story of your child as you envisioned it when he or she was born? Your road map to that beautiful gift is different from their Maker's. Is their shame on your journey?

The words "looking to Jesus, the founder and perfecter of our faith, who for the joy that was set before him endured the cross, despising the shame, and is seated at the right hand of the throne of God" (Hebrews 12:2) cause me to stop dead in my tracks and analyze my parental journey. Plainly, there have been parenting seasons disconnected from God's plans for my children's lives. I can choose to have the best of both worlds in the world of entanglements, or I can turn my eyes from all detours and fix them on Jesus to gain the power to run the race effectively.

It is always a joy to watch my people from Kenya run and win marathons. They do not carry huge suitcases or extra baggage. They do not browse the Web on their cell phones during the race. They drink only water to stay hydrated. To win, the marathoner has to endure to the end.

The author of Hebrews urges you and me, who are in this race of life, to consider the ultimate example of endurance: Jesus Christ. Jesus lived his earthly life by faith and humbly depended on God, the spring of power and secret of his peace. He endured the cross, determined to carry out the will of his Father in Gethsemane. He focused on the joy that was to come when he was resurrected and restored to glory with his Father, as it was in the beginning, and gave his life to save his sheep. Fix your eyes on him in faith. He is your destination!

Consider Gina's life. As an only child, she had an opportunity to live out the America dream by being accepted to a prestigious university at a young age. She had the spiritual, emotional, and financial support of many of her family members. All seemed to be going well, and she was excited for the opportunity ahead of her. She looked forward to an exciting and rewarding college experience and ultimately to a successful professional career, allowing her to bring change to her community and uplift her family.

Unfortunately, tragedy struck before her final school year, and she lost her life in a car accident. It was heartbreaking not only for her family but also for her community. Gina was a role model for her family members, and with her death, many were devastated. She had a promising life, but all was taken away from her. This untimely death led to health complications for her mother. How can a parent make sense out of this incomprehensible reality?

In another scenario, Kinto was born a healthy, bubbly child with a promising future. She was the joy for everyone in the village. She lit the room with laughter and brought so much fun to her family. Kinto had a heart of gold, loved beauty, pursued secretarial courses, and found a cosmetics career. She was a black-melanated beauty. In search of a happily ever after life, at twenty-two years old, she married a prominent businessman only to find herself in a trap of endless fights. Kinto encountered domestic violence and mental anguish. She was diagnosed in February with HIV and was dead by December of the same year. She left behind a daughter who was unable to make sense of a life with no mother and an absent father.

Grieving the death of a child does not ever get better. How could Gina's and Kinto's heartbroken parents make sense of these incomprehensible acts of God at such a prime age?

Gina and Kinto were believers in the Lord Jesus Christ. They served faithfully and brought so much joy to their parents, families, and communities. Many people doubted the families' abilities to cope after these losses. They assumed the worst and thought the families would be racked with mental and emotional anguish. Their parents had many sorrowful days and sleepless nights. Nothing could assuage their pain, and this resulted in barriers with other children and kin as they battled to make sense of this reality.

However, the question of why remains unanswered until we meet in eternity, as explained by Paul in his letter to the Corinthians: "Now we see but a poor reflection as in a mirror; then we shall know fully, even as I am fully known" (1 Corinthians 13:12). The apostle Paul clearly explained that as believers, we will not have full understanding until eternity. That implies we must learn to accept that partial understanding.

Some days Gina's mother cried when she looked at her daughter's picture. Her niece and nephews gave her reasons to live, but nothing compared to the satisfaction brought by one's child. Her relationship with God felt different. She was not able to pray or read the Bible. She had isolated herself from her closest friends, and her marriage was suffering. Her husband was hurting too and could not fill the void. Should a parent have to bury a child?

Scriptures tell us that God has given us all we need for life and godliness in Christ, including what we need for our parenting journeys.

Are these issues brought on by having weak faith or through sins? Why did the Lord say no to them or allow something bad to happen? Why? Does God not supersede our plans?

Kinto had a promising future and would have been a great mother to the only child, who now had many unanswered questions and was left to be raised by her grandfather. Kinto could have promoted unity in the family; met her community's emotional, moral, and spiritual needs; and expanded on the Great Commission globally. Kinto's dream was short-lived. She earned the nickname Explorer Beauty because she was always on the go and wanted to impact the world.

Parents, we do not just want a happy destination. We want to map out our journeys with vision boards and pen it off ourselves. As I write this book in the middle of a global pandemic, I am reminded of the uncertainties of life. The processes and journeys anticipated and written as New Year's resolutions may not bring the anticipated joy. Instead, there are sleepless nights with paralyzing emotional pain. I suspect you might have experienced his kind of journey.

We all have hope for a smooth process and are hopeful and prayerful for a great future. God, through his prophet Jeremiah, tells us, "For I know the plans I have for you, declares the Lord for welfare and not for evil to give you a future and a hope" (Jeremiah 29:11).

No one is immune to questioning life's outcomes. Why would a parent invest for better opportunities just to be struck by misfortune? Are there any parents who come out of these tragic situations where children have died or detoured? Is it a dream that we can pray away on a prayer line or with a sister or brother in Christ?

With the millions of amazing whys, my dear friends,

thousands of families come to mind who are devout Christians dedicated to spreading the Great Commission and who live by the dictates of scripture. They are not immune to the trials and tribulations and have had their share of suffering.

Tune went to nursing school, got married, and became a mother. She had to became a full-time housewife to take care of her twin daughters, who had a learning disability, and a troubled teenage son. At middle age, Tune succumbed to terminal cancer, leaving behind her husband with the three children. Tom, a successful businessman, could not cope with the demands of being a single father with no kin in a foreign land to assist him. He took the children back to his aging parents and relatives, back to his original home in East Africa. Tune and Tom had dreams of a healthy family. The double tragedy of the children's disability and the death of Tune, a loving mother and wife made no sense. Tom became depressed and lost his business. The twists and turns of life left his mother devasted, and she later developed high blood pressure and died of a stroke.

Mind you, so far the happenings are within families of believers in the Lord Jesus Christ who faithfully served the Lord. Even the most prudent ride the wheel of misfortune!

"Is This an Act of God?"

Let's unpack together and get a glimpse of our parenting world anchored in faith of God.

Might there be a misunderstanding about God? Is God obligated to explain himself to us? His promises are yes and amen, and they never return to him void. Proverbs 25:2 states, "It is the glory of God to conceal things, but the glory of kings is to search things out. As the heavens for height, and the earth for depth, so the heart of kings is unsearchable." Isaiah 40:18 says, "To whom then shall they liken God? or what likeness will you compare him to?"

Further, according to Acts 17:23, "He is the God of Scripture, alas the unknown God. God caused nothing outside of himself." And according to Ephesians 1:11, "He worketh all things after the counsel of His will, and he unsearchable things belong to Him."

As evidenced in Scripture, he is solitary in his majesty, unique in his excellency, and peerless in his perfections. Therefore man cannot comprehend or understand his attributes revealed in the holy Scriptures. The book of Exodus states, "Who is like unto thee, O Lord, among the gods? Who is like Thee, glorious in holiness, fearful in praises, doing wonders?" (Exodus 15:11).

"Why me? Why my child, Lord?" The many unanswered questions do not make sense with our human analysis. Our mental movie does not always takes us through a glorious outcome. A perfect formula of four plus four equals eight, but how about when the answer is far from the normal eight?

An example can be found from a story told by a close relative of a friend whose nephew drowned in a family swimming pool. They were also still moaning about the death of their father-in-law. Was this a curse from the ancestors, as some bond by cultural chains still believe, or was it anger from God from secret sins? It is hard to comprehend. But we know the truth for those in the light from the letter of Paul to the Galatians: "Christ redeemed us from the curse of the law by becoming a curse for us—for it is written, 'Cursed is everyone who is hanged on a tree'" (Galatians 3:13). Believers in the faith of Jesus Christ are justified and find favor with God and are not bound by human traditions and beliefs. This issue will be continued in a later chapter.

My child in the backseat asking if we are there yet is not alone. In life's journey, we want to take the pilot seat and navigate our parental plane to our expected destination with a smooth ride, avoiding the turbulence. But a glorious outcome is absolutely not possible without our almighty God in the equation

Parental Foundation

An unknown God cannot be trusted, served, or worshipped. Therefore, our family and parental foundations ought to be on the foundation of the factual knowledge of God and anchored to his promises. We must allow his will, not our will or alternative benefit—which get in the way of answered prayers—or else we will miss the blessing in the storm.

The wisest man who ever lived, Solomon, wrote in the book of Ecclesiastes, "And as you do not know the path of the wind, or how the body is formed in a mother's womb, so you cannot understand the work of God" (Ecclesiastes 11:5). A more theoretical understanding of God is needed for believers in the Lord Jesus Christ and enables us to take up parents' roles successfully. It requires submission to His authority, yielding to Him, and regulating parenting roles and every detail to his precepts and commandments.

Is the eternal and infinite God within the grasp of human reason? In his gospel, John states, "God is a spirit" (John 4:24). Therefore God can only be known spiritually, and not even the intellect can understand him.

Is spiritual knowledge fully understood? Absolutely no. The regenerated soul has to grow in the grace and the experience of our Lord and Savior Jesus Christ (2 Peter 3:18). Christian parents' prayer and aim should be "'to walk in a manner worthy of the Lord, fully pleasing to him,' bearing fruit in every good work and increasing in the knowledge of God" (Colossians 1:10).

When I gave my life to Christ, I assumed that was the end of any suffering, and life was full of hallelujah and amen. There is no expectation that suffering, trial, and tribulations are part of the "salvation package." The ABCs—accept, believe, and confess—are well-meaning, but there are occasions in the parenting journey where things do not go according to plan. Even after you have done your best and dedicated your child to the Lord like Hannah, you realize that the choices and changes in your child are a lifelong process, despite the desire to pray it away.

John 3:16 states, "For God, so loved the world that He gave His One and only son, that whosoever believes in Him should not perish but have eternal life." It is a well-meaning verse and an excellent plan and confession when we respond and acknowledge Jesus as Lord God. You want him to be the Lord of your life, a golden list, accepted and justified but not complete due to the presence of sin, daily transformed and conforming to the image of Christ. The subject of sin is elaborated on in the next chapter.

The parenting journey has hills and valleys, with teachable unfinished moments. "You will have trials and tribulations in this world but be of good cheer because I have overcome the world" (John 16:33). That is the gospel, and parents, as believers in the Lord Jesus Christ, need preparation for the uncertainty of life with a certain God. Apostle Paul states it clearly: "But I received mercy for this reason, that in me, as the foremost, Jesus Christ might display his perfect patience as an example to those who were to believe in him for eternal life" (1 Timothy 1:16). An illustration of our heavenly Father's patience and the same need for your children, but the need for easy solutions gets you and me as parents in deep melancholy and introspection.

To Erick and Paul, the Lord's faithful servants, the grand plan means a bed-bound son who has six months to live. The parents are devastated with no guidance during the critical time. Not even a prayer from a hospice chaplain can answer the question, "Why should I have to bury my child?"

For Jill, it is sheer agony when she cannot afford chemotherapy, has no coverage for healthcare problems, goes to the emergency room—and the physician cannot see her. Her the child succumbs to glioblastoma, a rare form of brain cancer.

Lucy, you cannot be depicting God as senseless and uncaring to his beloved! Are there double standards in his kingdom?

The scriptures are clear concerning the nature of God. "God is light" (1 John1:5), the opposite of darkness. Darkness elaborated is evil, sin, and death; light stands for goodness, life, and holiness.

God is light and means God is excellent, and all His ways require a total surrender to His will, parenting included! But how is this possible? The Holy Spirit reveals these truths, which cannot be found by human understanding and searching alone. John's gospel teaches, "I still have many things to say to you, but you cannot bear them now. When the Spirit of Truth comes, he will guide you into all the Truth, for he will not speak on his authority, but whatever he hears he will speak, and he will declare to you the things that are to come. He will glorify Me, for he will take what is mine and declare it to you. The Father has abundance; therefore, I said that he would take mine and report it to you" (John 16:12–15)

Parenting Experience and Circumstances

In my parenting journey and as a biblical counselor, the encounters of wayward children and parents in pain is not foreign. I have experienced hardship and heartbreak with unfathomable pain. There have been millions of unexplainable sorrowful, trying seasons with different forms and fashions from all races and tribes worldwide. These include drug addiction, alcohol and substance abuse, teen and young adult suicide, teen pregnancy, and debilitating premature death of children, including recent child deaths from the COVID-19 pandemic.

Why does a loving God permit such evils and suffering to the good and the bad?

It is common to be frustrated with God in times of crisis, especially when the parenting journey takes a downward spiral in the valley, a period of prolonged dry bones, famine, raging fires, storms, and repeated hurricanes of life, contrary to biblical teaching and human understanding.

With the outcome contrary to the expectation as devastating as a child's death, substance abuse, mental illness, or a life-changing encounter, this can lead to unrighteous anger, bitterness, depression, and a sense of rejection. The pain and suffering experienced do not respect anyone.

Here are some questions from believers and nonbelievers in Christ.

Dear Ms. Lucy,

Being a single mom and watching my daughter strung out on drugs, sleeping on the streets is not easy. I lost my son through suicide last year. This makes no sense!

Dear Lucy,

There have been days being a dad has been hard, let alone also having to be her mum, since the mother is fighting stage four cervical cancer, and I still have to figure out life in a wheelchair from a car accident as a person with paraplegia.

As parents, I understand we should be the trees that shelter and nurture the fruit of our wombs, but regarding taking a different path, it's a challenge to pull it together without much sense. A child's unexpected detour can lead to a parent's fleshly reaction along the lines of anger, disgust, sadness, and some depression or mental anguish, with no fruit of the spirit contrary to the faith.

Scripture clarifies that "His divine power has given us everything we need for a godly life through our knowledge of him who called us by his glory and goodness" (2 Peter 1:3). How can one explain that a daughter's or son's waywardness is not a result of weak faith or sin, causing God's wrath? Is there any purpose in this detour?

For Mary, the mother of Jesus, detours were not strangers or ugly incidences. The Son was born in a manager, lost in the temple for days, beaten, and rejected. He suffered, sweated blood, and eventually was crucified with thieves. For Joseph in the Bible, in the Old Testament story, life was being tossed in a pit, wrongfully imprisoned, forgotten, and dismissed. That is the undeniable truth in Joseph's story: that intended evil becomes eventual good in God's hands. You meant evil against me, but God meant it for good, to bring it about so that many people are kept alive as they are today (Genesis 50:20). In thriving, my fellow parent is not only surviving in the face of adversity, calamity, pandemic, or parenting; God will use it for good. But how? In all these unpredicted paths, God's plan is studied and displayed.

Not Weak Faith

Many parents have fallen into this trap of the satanic lie, lack of knowledge, and understanding of scriptural truth. They are rooted in spiritual ignorance and fear, which is the absolute opposite of faith. Trials and tribulations are part of the walk of a believer, but exegesis of scripture is important, rather than taking a scripture and running with it. In his last words, Jesus gave a great commission his disciples: "Then He opened their minds to understand the scriptures" (Luke 24:45). The instructions are weighty, with a mighty task charged to Jesus's followers. Think of the privilege and responsibility of telling the good news of the eternal life and forgiveness of sins to those who admit, believe, and confess.

Do your children know about what Jesus Christ has done for them?

Do you know what he is doing through you as a parent?

Can you afford to deprive your children of having the good news to make a choice?

For many years, I envisioned going on missions to other continents and countries as the great commission. Wrong! The good news starts with me and you in our homes. Spread it to the community. Your prayers and financial gifts can help spread the good news to the world!

Remember that it starts with you, Mom! It starts with you, Dad!

Double-Minded

A double mind is having opposite opinions or opposing views at different times. The Bible says, "He is a double-minded man is unstable in all his ways" (James 1:8).

Unfortunately, as a Christian parent and a lesson to many, it is easy to fall prey to an unstable mind, find no meaning, lose joy in the journey of parenting, and see no light at the end of the tunnel. Still, some face shattered dreams filled with murmurings, selfish pleas, and depression over the detours of their children, ignorantly not knowing that regardless of how one feels, God holds the future of our children.

Though pain and suffering are a source of mental anguish, our unstable minds shred our faith. A cause for this is an unsound mind. God is immutable, unchanging in His character, promises, and will. His wisdom, holiness, justice, goodness, and truth are infinite, eternal, and unchangeable. Repetition is good for the soul and learning God's unchanging character. Say and believe it, as in the words of Paul to the Romans: "And we know that for those who love God all things work together for good for those who are called according to his purpose" (Romans 8:28). Say it even when the situation makes no sense.

What is essential in your parental journey? Is it the education, accolades, and certificates of your child? Jesus would call this short-sighted, as Apostle Peter emphasizes the Christian myopia that may warrant spiritual spectacles for a stronger Christian parenting, which overflows to the child no matter the outcome. "For whoever lacks these qualities is so nearsighted that he is blind, having forgotten that he was cleansed from his former sins" (2 Peter 1:9).

Sadly, Christian parents who are unstable and lose hope face greater devastation than nonbelievers who have no expectations. In times of crisis, out of the hope that God provides, our faith and love need to be biblically expressed, responding and understanding biblically to problems for the ultimate goal of glorifying God and allowing ourselves to be further conformed to the image of Jesus Christ. As Solomon states it, the wisest man who lived said, "Trust in the Lord with all your heart and lean not on your understanding; in all your ways submit to him, and he will make your paths straight" (Proverbs 3:5–6).

Seldom do we, as Christian parents and within our church communities, admit that our lights have been dimmed. It is not always well or okay. We emotionally deny that children do not meet our expectations and dreams and perceive the problems only at the feeling levels, allowing emotions to overrule us while not understanding the full scope of the problem and examining our perceptions in the light of God's word. These distressing feelings result in sin, as the psalmist states:

> There is no soundness in my flesh because of your indignation; there is no health in my bones because of my sin. For my iniquities have gone over my head; like a heavy burden, they are too heavy for me. My wounds stink and fester because of my foolishness, I am utterly bowed down and frustrated; all the day I go about mourning. For my sides are filled with burning, and there is no soundness in my flesh. I am feeble and crushed; It groans because of the tumult of my heart. O Lord, all my longing is before you; my weighing is not hidden from you. My heart throbs; my strength fails me, and the light of my eyes—it also has gone from me. (Psalm 38:3–10)

The anguish of the parent, the self-centered life, portrays God as distant, unloving, and unkind. The anger and arrogance are demonstrated by saying unkind words, shouting at the children, being overly critical, and letting the emotions take a toll. This leads to unnecessary physical symptoms that scourge our entities, such as depression, high blood pressure, cancer, and mental illness. Does this happen in parents who are believers in the Lord Jesus Christ? True! I am explaining a path and road I have traveled with a lot more of us.

Here are the words of a mother in mental anguish: "This cannot be happening to me. This does not make sense. I am a good mother in my own eyes. I went to church religiously, memorized or crammed scriptures, accorded the same to my children, was active and served, and gave tithes and offerings." Good parents deserve an excellent, sensible answer. Right?

God's Redemption at Life's Crossroads

A perfect example of Job's life in his trials explains a parental mental anguish: Talk of an honorable, God-fearing man of integrity. "There was a man in the land of Uz whose name was Job, and that man was blameless and upright, one who feared God and turned away from evil" (Job 1:1). The Devil dared Job's Faith: "And the LORD said to Satan, 'Behold, all that he has is in your hand. Only against him do not stretch out your hand.' So Satan went out from the presence of the LORD" (Job 1:12).

Talk about major trouble that is unavoidable in one day. Calamity pounced on Job. If there is a college of hard knocks for parents, Job may have been a pioneer. This is well illustrated in the book of Job:

> Now there was a day when his sons and daughters were eating and drinking wine in their oldest brother's house, and there came a messenger to Job ... While he was yet speaking, there came another and said, "The fire of God fell from heaven and burned up the sheep and the servants and consumed them, and I alone have escaped to tell you." While he was yet speaking, there came another and said, "The Chaldeans formed three groups and made a raid on the camels and took them and struck down the servants with

the edge of the sword, and I alone have escaped to tell you." While he was yet speaking, there came another and said, "Your sons and daughters were eating and drinking wine in their oldest brother's house, and behold, a great wind came across the wilderness and struck the four corners of the house, and it fell upon the young people, and they are dead, and I alone have escaped to tell you. (Job 1:13–19)

So how does our pain in parenting fit in God's plan?

According to my assumptions, I want to write the story of my parenting journey to relinquish control to an omniscient God. You may agree or not, make sense of it or not, but God knows everything. The events and lives of our children are past, present, and the future, and He is acquainted with every detail, as Daniel states: "He reveals deep and hidden things; he knows what is in the darkness, and the light dwells with him" (Daniel, 2:22). This is emphasized by the psalmist: "Such knowledge is too wonderful for me; it is high; I cannot attain it" (Psalm 139:6).

Our difficulty as parents lies in not knowing where to find true meaning in our journey. We would strip God of His omniscience with our carnal minds if we could, as proven in Romans 8:7. "The carnal mind is enmity with God" is a solemn fact, and no person can hide anything from him. The book of Ezekiel states that all that arises in your mind, imagination, and heart is known by God: "For I know the things that come into your mind, every one of them" (Ezekiel 11:5).

Parenting then becomes a journey of discovering the truth of God's Word and aligning with it in our thoughts and actions. But what is this truth? Can you have the truth with no power? God gives us both his Word and grace, which is his power and favor.

For me and most of my generation, boarding schools were the norm and worked for us. The three months away from home before a month break between semesters was a long time. Facing my parents with a report card or progress report was the most anticipated or dreadful moment. When my report card was good, I looked forward to the homegoing, but if it was bad, I felt the wrath of my dad even before I got home. I was afraid! My mother hand encouraged me to excel in my public speaking talents and provided a sense of safety from the wrath of my father. I felt the freedom to express my thoughts, and I remember speaking and dancing in front of guests at our home at a young age without fear. I had an urge to succeed in whatever I did, and I was equipped with the tools enabled by my parents' encouragement. I did struggle with some subjects, but the freedom and encouragement to excel in my gift came from my mother. I excelled at public speaking, and although my father was well meaning in his initial opposition, he realized my talents later and encouraged me. My report card improved, and my homecoming from sophomore year in high school was pleasant.

The combination of grace and truth brings desired results.

I later joined the school choir, with a perfect key of soprano. The combination of the vocal ranges from other choir members of tenor, alto, and others made an incredible mass choir, and the songs, written by our dedicated music teacher and choir mass, was reckoned with at the music festivals.

We can equate our parental roles to a song God has written for us to sing in the perfect key. Are you singing in the right key? Are you letting God direct some of the orchestra, or are you allowing him to be in full control? If you let him, he will produce a symphony, and his music will take over your soul. This music will move you to dance, which might seem to be insane to those who do not hear the music, but it is joy to the soul, as the Apostle Paul told the Corinthians: "For the word of the cross is folly to those who are perishing but to us who are being saved it is the power of God" (1 Corinthians 1:18).

Living Out Your Call

During the pandemic days, as I wrote this book when most things did not make sense and lots of uncertainties, my love for flowers and landscaping was reignited. In my search for more knowledge of which flowers bloom in the summer, planting the beautiful pansies, violas, snowdrops, hellebores, and any other winter-related flowers would make no sense. In some seasons of parenting in your pain and hard realities, be obedient and live out your calling! It is a season, it will pass.

2

Detours

> Detours are delays, and they have rerouted paths
> that keep us from our original route.
> —Dr. Tony Evans

I wish I could say that my parenting journey is a smooth ride. I wish I could say there have been no speed bumps.

I wish I could say my journey has had no yields or stop signs. I wish my parental GPS would not announce any detours for any of my parental journeys ahead. My mental vision board is well mapped out. I wish I could say I have never thought that God gave me a gift of the womb that could have been meant for someone else or another family. I wish I could hear my mind say, "Rerouting—make a U-turn." I wish my heart would be satisfied in counting my blessings one by one rather than assessing and analyzing deeply the path taken.

These are my wishes, but they are not reflections of the parent I am today. Disappointment lurks in my heart due to the "normal and perfect parenting" that resides in me. But do we live in that perfect world? The reason my perfect motherly instincts kick in is because we let God take the driver's seat and co-journey with him to make the imperfections perfect.

What is the purpose of these detours? Why does the Bible speak so strongly about rejoicing in our afflictions, in our detours? Or is it our path to hope, as an apostle wrote in a letter to the Romans: "Not only that, but we rejoice in our suffering produces endurance, and endurance produces character, and character produces hope, and hope does not put us to shame, because God's love has been poured into our hearts through the Holy Spirit who has been given to us" (Romans 5:3–5).

Family Dynamics

My first rodeo came with a rude awakening, and this left me wondering whether the parental battle was for my family alone. Or are battles faced by all families? The physical nature of the struggle made no sense at all. As I struggled to figure out the detour taken, it became increasingly difficult, and I asked God to open my eyes to the spiritual reality behind a child's future on the dark verge of life.

The detour and its effects negatively affected me as a mother. The siblings struggled with unanswered questions. The Witness of the downward spiral of loved ones, and family members are uniquely involved. It is not limited to emotional distress, legal problems, impaired attachment, and relationships.

Detours affect family dynamics and pose a danger to the family system. The high negative impacts of detours may be bad choices of friends and flare tempers substance abuse, different sexual orientation, loss and disruption of communication, finances, and social life routines can lead to dysfunctional families characterized by an environment of secrecy, loss, conflict, violence, emotional chaos, and fear.

The parental challenges and impact affect the whole family, who have little or no knowledge for appropriate interventions. Oh, the agony of detours!

How about when she prays and fasts day in day out, speaks a blessing over her child, but is not sure if a sheriff will knock on her door to identify her daughter? The heartbroken mother wails, broken up, and states, "I have been adapting other people's children. My daughter has become a disgrace to me and the community." She does not know what to do. This is mental anguish. Is God silent?

I do not want us to deny our humanity of a bumpy or rerouted parental journey. To express the disillusionment, anger, and fears is to be human. Let your focus be on what God says, not what you think or your feelings. Acknowledge him as the Potter. As parents, we cannot journey without God's touch. We are transformed by renewing our minds with his Word.

Storms

I have had numerous storm seasons with severe hurricanes in the state of Texas, where everything is "big." We experienced Hurricane Katrina when our daughter was only four months old. We were strangers in the land, having made an Abrahamic move of faith to a different state. We drove for sixteen hours to a place for a one-hour meet with strangers, who entertained us and later became family friends.

I recall my late father-in-law asking my husband and me, "Do you have to stay in that place with so many storms, year after year?" The verse that immediately came to mind was from the book of Numbers: "And the people spoke against Moses, 'Why have you brought us up out of Egypt to die in the wilderness? For there is no food and no water, and we loathe this worthless food'" (Numbers 21:5).

Storms push us outside our comfort zones. Storms expose both weaknesses and latent opportunities. As I write, in the last few months during the pandemic, COVID-19 has shaken relationships and redefined man people's way of doing business. Storms reveal the foundation of a family, marriage, parenting, career, or business. Storms tell what material you and I are made of. The coronavirus has wreaked havoc in families, communities, global economies, and more. There are increasing cases of depression, domestic violence, and suicide, causing suffering globally while families battle post–COVID-19 effects. It is a good example of an unforeseen storm of life with many spiritual, economic, and health questions.

Apostle Paul stated, "I am acting with great boldness toward you: I am filled with comfort. In all our affliction, I am overflowing with joy. For even when we came into Macedonia, our bodies had no rest, but we were afflicted at every turn-fighting without and fear within" (Corinthians 7:4–5).

Note the disappointment and discouragement of a parent feeling defeated and a failure. Lucy, did you say a failure? I'm born-again, Spirit-filled, faithfully serving, staunch Christian. Parents, are you currently facing a similar state, with your child in unfathomable pain? Does it feel like an intensive care unit of poor choices, defiance, disobedience, and unwanted pregnancy? Is the child in prison or rehabilitation? Is there a life-debilitating situation or a disability? Is there an amber alert as you read this book, and you distressed beyond your imagination? The parental outcome will not always be as you anticipate. Scripture says, "Beloved, do not be surprised at the fiery trial when it comes upon you to test you *as though something strange was happening to you*" (1 Peter 4:12; emphasis added).

Are you feeling unsettled and do not know why? The trials or situations can cause a well-meaning Christian to get into an emotional tailspin. You are beloved by God, and you are dear to him. The strange trials and persecutions are not for your destructions but are exercise for your grace.

In my current residence, the mayhem that a hurricane unleashed on us didn't come from just the sky but was also on the ground. It swept in from the Waton Prairie, some thirty miles west of downtown, causing a crisis storm barrier. So many lives were lost, and people drowned in a raging storm and rising waters. The detours of your child, the death of your child, and the debilitating situation may leave you feeling drowned in discouragement with an absent or silent God, and you have no answers for your questions: "Why my child? Where is God? When will He answer my plea?"

I could write many books of all the incidences that left me in a well of dejection and despair, to the point where I was demoralized to face specific dreams with crushed faith. In my biblical counseling years, I have witnessed parents' experiences as they are crushed in spirit and are to the point of despair. These storms are real in our eyes, but you cannot overcome by your own strength. The unpredictable path of a child's destiny can leave one with a misunderstanding of God and leave one to feel unloved by him. This is not the abundant life of a parent that God intended for us. It is contrary to his promises to meet our parenting pressures and demands on our terms or to rely on our human strength. It is futile and a heavy burden, and it is not worth carrying.

The scriptures are explicit with examples of men and women who are troubled. A good example is Moses: "Then Moses turned to the Lord and said, 'O Lord, why have you done evil to these people? Why did you ever send me? For since I came to Pharaoh to speak in your name, he has done evil to these people, and you have not delivered your people at all'" (Exodus 5:22–23). Have we not fallen into the same trap as Moses and misunderstood God in his plan and purpose for you, your children, and your family? However, Moses did not buy into the devil's tricks, and he contended for his faith and walked in the promises of God to lead the Israelites through the wilderness.

Mental Anguish and Pain of Children's Detour

You may know what it is to wait upon the expectation of a child's dream to flourish—and then feel disillusioned and hurt due to the crisis barrier of rebellion, suicide, drugs, alcohol, and substance abuse. You feel an abandonment by God, affecting your faith with bitterness and anger.

But is this abandonment? It is a terrible lie that alienates believers from their loving Father at the prime age of parenting teenagers with promising futures. From the fleshly perspective, one expectation can feel like a cutoff. But from a spiritual perspective, we know the expectation of the righteous shall not be cut off. From a human perspective, this does not make sense. Let us see the truth of God's Word as stated in the book of Proverbs: "For indeed there is an end, and thine expectation shall not be cut off" (Proverbs 23:18). What a great promise! Even when we don't see it or feel it, God is still working! Your trials and the sinner's prosperity will soon end. The prayer to your child, and the biblical and blessings of God's instructions, are seeds that will yield fruits.

Insufficient

Most of us parents have dreams of functional families with our children having rosy lives, different aspirations, and glorious futures. *Recognizing what you are unable to do is essential to good parenting.* Yes, God's *will is* for families to flourish, prosper, and possess the land, including taking a leap of faith to migrate to a land filled with milk and honey after countless nights of prayer and fasting. But you should recognize that not every plan will go your way.

How do you and I respond when we realize the outcome is different and insufficient? What is success? There are times and seasons when we honestly need the undiluted word and are challenged with biblical wisdom with careful prayer. Making the Abrahamic move from the known land to the unknown land of opportunity comes with great expectations of a glorious journey, but it is not without pauses. To say it is a bed of roses would be a lie. The disillusionment takes a toll on the family emotionally. The struggle lingers on from what it could have been to what it is. You will agree with me that this uninvited guest is emotionally draining.

The life of your child is not what you envisioned and crafted in your mental vision board. Worse still, what do you tell that curious auntie or uncle, or the community? "Ms. Lucy, how are you? How are the children? What grade are they in again? Has Caesar completed college? How is Nathaniel and Jonathan? Oh, and how is young princess Rosalia?" In my heart, I felt sufficient as a good and faithful speaker about the skeleton in the closet, and not even a prosecutor would doubt my motives. But does a parent's reaction define one's love for the child? Absolutely not. In most cases, the bond is strong, but the storms affects parent-child relationships. Insufficient parenting tools shape parenting style, and the problem escalates. The hurling accusations, raising voice, and worse still yelling in anticipation for instant change of the situation do more harm than good.

Living a life of faith and experiencing drastic detours from a child does not make sense without spiritual spectacles. But by now, we understand the possible reality for believers in the Lord Jesus Christ. Trials are part of the salvation package and the disillusionment of a gift from God, though it may not feel like a gift at all at that moment. That might ease the question of, "Why my child?" It reminds us of Paul's comforting words to the Corinthians: "No temptation has overtaken you except what is common to humankind. And God is faithful; he will not let you be tempted, beyond what you can bear. But when you are tempted, he will also provide a way out so that you can endure it" (1 Corinthians 10:13).

Hundreds of thousands of parents have their children's destinies cut off. There is grieving over a wayward child, dysfunctional families, marriages breaking due to conflict in bringing up children, children taking different faiths from their parents, or children having no faith at all. Consider Gideon's life. At seventeen years of age, he migrated on admission to an Ivy League school. The motto "Harambee" (unity) of the community raised millions of shillings to send their bright village son to further his education. In return, he was to go back and transform his village. It would be a commitment of three and a half years, but at the end of the third year, Gideon drove his car off a cliff. Gideon's body could not be identified. He had wounds on his head and a note on his dashboard. The senseless death of a promising young life set the family back in his native land, and the community was in disbelief.

The parents were staunch Christians with their children. They served at their local church as deacons and elders. They sacrificed their goats, cattle, and title deeds for a shiny future. To receive such a blow does not make sense! Gideon's mother was in disbelief. Her blood sugars and blood pressure were uncontrollable and led to a stroke. It affected her speech, and she could no longer lead the woman's Christian group in her church. Sylvia, the younger son, could not cope with his only brother's death, whom he looked up to. Sylvia became a habitual drunkard and dropped out of school in the third year of high school. Their only daughter of sixteen years was disabled and struggled with debilitating mental illness symptoms, and her primary caregiver was the mother, who was now bedridden.

The father, the only breadwinner, became sad, disgusted, and angry. Even though Mr. Patrick professed Christ as Savior, his life was a mixture of family problems, shame, suffering, and estranged behavior from his faith family. Before the crisis struck, the church in which the family was involved did not respond to the deacon and the family when he requested some church members pray over them. The support and comfort they needed were not there. The pastor and other deacons were simply not equipped to get a complete handle on the family.

The man fell away from the church but continued to pray at home, with a handful of relatives visiting him occasionally and helping with house and farm chores. Scripture tells us in 1 Peter 2:3, "If indeed you have tasted that the Lord is good."

The lack of knowledge of both essential function and scriptural truth causes more strain on families and parents. Over the years, children's lives have been destroyed by drugs and mental anguish. In some communities, sadly mental illness in a believer's home is equated to weak faith, demon possession, or generational sin. But the good news is revealed in the scriptures of Apostle Paul: "Christ redeemed us from the curse of the law by becoming a curse for us—for is written, 'Cursed is everyone who hanged on a tree'" (Galatians 1:13).

The church's lack of understanding of mental illness, rooted in spiritual ignorance and fear, leaves the congregations or the parents suffering in pain with no place of refuge. Yet the pastors or clergy are the first places people run to. Where do we run to in our hard realities of parental journey?

The once prestigious, now dysfunctional family of Patrick became city gossip with a call to "get their house in order" from a session of counseling. They became a symbol of shame and a laughingstock in the community. They were angry with themselves and God. In such instances, who is to blame?

You may be internalizing the same disillusionment, and you have no place to hide your face in the community. You are exhausted with sleepless nights and stressed beyond stretch of your imagination. My dear friend, the disillusionment may be an eye-opener to the steadfast love of God without shame, leaning on His promises. You may not feel or see it, but remember that we operate on faith of the word of God. Here is a command by Apostle Paul in the book of Romans: "For I am not ashamed of the gospel, for it is the power of God for salvation to everyone who believes ... For in it the righteousness of God is revealed from Faith to Faith as it is written 'The righteous shall live by Faith'" (Romans 1:117).

Death of a Child

Suffering the devastating loss of a child can lead to parents feeling lost and alone in their grief. In my biblical counseling and crisis care nurse experiences, several pleas from parents left me with many unanswered burning questions.

Words of Comfort to a Grieving Parent

Put your faith and trust in God and know that he will never abandon you. Let his Word comfort you in moments of despair. Find joy in his promise that you will one day be reunited with your child in heaven. Were these words well received? Do they make sense during the loss and grieving period?

Wisdom

It has been a long journey of fighting and discerning human wisdom or total submission to Godly wisdom, love, and dedication with grace. Isn't parenting with grace and wisdom all you need?

> The Spirit searches all things, even God's deep things. For who knows a person's thoughts except their Spirit within them? In the same way, no one knows the thoughts of God except the Spirit of God. What we have received is not the Spirit of the world, but the Spirit who is from God, so that we may understand what God has freely given us. This is what we speak, not in words taught us by human wisdom but in words led by the Spirit, explaining spiritual realities with Spirit-taught words. The person without the Spirit does not accept the things that come from the Spirit of God but considers them foolishness and cannot understand them because they are discerned only through the Spirit. The person with the Spirit makes judgments about all things, but such a person is not subject to merely human judgments.
> (1 Corinthians 2:10–15)

Comforting Verses for Loss of a Child

Jesus said to her, "I am the resurrection and the Life. The one who believes in me will live, even though they die; and whoever lives by believing in me will never die. Do you believe this?" (John 11:25–26)

For this light momentary affliction is preparing for us an eternal weight of glory beyond all comparison, as we look not to the things that are seen but to the things that are unseen. For the things that are seen are transient, but the things that are unseen are eternal. (2 Corinthians 4:17–18)

He will wipe away every tear from their eyes, and death shall be no more, neither shall there be mourning, nor crying, nor pain anymore, for the former things have passed away. (Revelation 21:4)

Fear not, for I am with you; be not dismayed, for I am your God. I will strengthen you, I will help you. I will uphold you with my righteous right hand. (Isaiah 41:10)

Let not your hearts be troubled. Believe in God; also believe in me. In Father's house are many rooms; if it were not so, would I have told you that I go to prepare a place for you? And if I go and prepare a place for you, I will come again and will take you to myself, that where I am you may be also. And You know the way to where I am going. (John 14:1–4)

Destruction of Life

Like David, who hid in the cave while running from Saul, I have run from an imaginary Saul, from the adverse outcomes of my children's choices. We face times of discouragement and disappointment. But does the discouragement hold your thoughts back by meditating on God's goodness and faithfulness, leading you to an imaginary road trip and painting the road of your other children in the same light? The deception of the enemy can thrive in our minds to believe the eyes of the flesh rather than dive into God's promises and final say. All God expects of you is to enter into his rest while journeying through parenting with grace, creating an atmosphere of steadfast love.

As earlier stated, the mind does go through a road trip on bumpy roads on the parenting journey. You and I know the voice driving this trip is not of God. It is Satan, the author and father of deception. As Apostle John states, "You are of your father, the Devil, and your will is to do your father's desires. He was a murderer from the beginning and does not stand in the truth, because there is no truth in him. When he lies, he speaks out of his own character, for he is a liar and the father of lies" (John 8:44). The Word of God puts us in perspective. God's truth and his Word empower us and renew our thoughts, but the devil, the author of lies, wants to confuse us.

My friend, put that faith on the shelf. You will need it. Stars are best seen in the dark. God lets us know the glares of the dark.

> The Lord GOD has given me the tongue of those taught that I may know how to sustain with a word him who is weary. Morning by morning, he awakens; he awakens my ear to hear as those who are taught. (Isaiah 50:4)

> For I consider that the sufferings of this present time are not worth comparing with the glory that is to be revealed in us. (Romans 8:18)

Amid your sorrow, it is possible to experience the peace and comfort of Christ. With brothers and sisters, there is fellowship (Koinonia), praying for God's comfort, and plugging into the community of believers. Hurricane-force winds require exceptional parenting skills that begin with this plea: "God, I don't know what to do." As the Bible says, "We don't know what to do, but our eyes are on you" (2 Chronicles 20:12b). Let's hit the pause button on this topic; we will discuss our wailing help in a later chapter.

As parents, we are found between a rock and a hard place with basic but profound requests and with an underlying spiritual diagnosis. The Lord has placed in our midst men and women of God to stand in our gap when we need prayers, as stated by Apostle Paul: "Epaphras, who is one of you, a servant of Christ Jesus, greets you, always struggling on your behalf in his prayers, that you may stand mature and fully assured in all the will of God. For I bear him witness that he has worked hard for you and for those in Laodicea and in Hierapolis" (Colossian 4:12–13)

By nature, parents are confident, skilled, and battle-tested. So often we roll out of bed and start leading the charge. It is easy to wake up, survey the landscape, and immediately focus on solving problems, creating opportunities, and marshaling the troops. Ultimately, a parent is only as durable as the humility that undergirds them—the humility that drives them first to seek help from the Lord.

We do not always have the liberty to call our families to seek God corporately. However, every parent does have the opportunity to daily, privately, seek heaven's help. We need war rooms in our closets—praying closets to fervently pray, travail, and wail to our Father! "Thus says the LORD of hosts: 'Consider, and call for the mourning women to come, end for the skillful women to come; let them make haste and raise a wailing over us, that our eyes may run down with tears and our eyelids flow with water. For a sound of wailing is heard from Zion: "How we are ruined!"'" (Jeremiah 9:17–19). In the New International Version and some other versions, it is the "wailing women." In my counselling sessions and speaking engagements, in times of mourning I do not shy away from saying tears are healthy. The hallmark of every great parent is the ability to lead oneself. This means facing your limitations and leaning on God. We teach and parent best by allowing God to lead us and guide us. Be like Jesus. Pray like Jesus. There will be more discussion on prayer in later chapters.

> Early in the morning, shall I seek you! O God, you are my God; earnestly I seek you; my soul thirsts for you; my flesh faints for you, as in a dry and weary land where there is no water. (Psalm 63:1)

Suffering

Does God owe us an apology for the parental pain and suffering? Dive deeply in his Word of encouragement and look at Apostle Peter. Peter is my to go-to apostle in parental pain and suffering—and also joy. This can be acquitted to a breath of fresh air as he explains the coexistence of pain, sorrow, and sobriety: "Beloved, do not be surprised at the fiery ordeal when it comes upon you to test you, as though something strange was happening to you. But rejoice in so far as you share Christ's sufferings, that you may be also rejoice and be glad when his glory is revealed" (1 Peter 4:12–13). Let us gladly receive the pain of discouragement and embrace the love and hope promised.

For a moment, let's hit the pause button on the whys of parental pain. Let us reexamine ourselves and be equipped with revelation, knowledge, and wisdom.

3

God Makes Sense

What comes into our minds when we think about
God is the most important thing about us.
—A. W. Tozer

It is a human response to ask and wonder what is going on around us, but when we start to doubt God's sovereignty, that is a problem. I paraphrase from a favorite quote below.

> It is hard to know where to begin making sense. Is there any sense? Solemnity and awe should garner our approach to the question—the deep humility which is appropriate in the presence of the profound. For some people's parents right now, concluding for abandonment seems like the obvious thing to do; the kind of suffering which has come with substance abuse, mental breakdown, suicides, and many more catastrophic events in families seems incompatible with the existence of a loving God. Yet our conviction that we have been face-to-face with real good and real evil and the unpalatability of there being no

meaning at all suggests we cannot remove God from the picture. To remove God from the image is to remove the possibility of an answer.

—Andy Moore

Master Planner

Since the beginning of the world, our sovereign God had a master plan and seasons for you and your child. King David states in Psalms 139:15–16, "My frame was not hidden from you, when I was being made in secret, intricately woven in the depths of the earth. Your eyes saw my unformed substance, in your book were written, every one of them, the days that were formed for me, when as yet there none of them."

Your relationship with your child, family, or anyone is determined by your relationship with the giver of life, the master planner, as written in the gospel of John: "All things were made through him, and without him was not any thing made that was made. In him was life, and the life was the light of men" (John 1:3–4).

Is that not true for your child too? As parents, we are attached to outcomes. We read God's promises, know the truth, and verbalize. But let us be honest: when things go contrary to our expectations, we get on a rollercoaster of doubts. But as a parent for some decades or more, you may have come to the revelation that it is unbelievably powerful when you decide to trust in God instead of relying on your understanding of things. "Trust in the LORD with all your heart, and do not lean on your own understanding In all your ways acknowledge him, and he will make straight your paths" (Proverbs 3:5–6). It is our human that nature when things are going well, we can easily sense God's closeness. But even on our worst days, if we sit with him for a while, he will not only comfort us through the pain we are feeling, but he will also give us a fresh parental perspective so that we can begin to see things from his point of view.

Yield, stop, and look around you. Where can you see God's goodness in your parenting journey? What can you thank him for? This is still an excellent motivator for parenting; it is the gift of the womb! There are different talents and joys that each child brings. Looking back, I could not have asked for more than the gift of three loving sons and my adorable daughter. You cannot be too familiar with Scripture, and it is the revelation and illumination that makes sense, not human understanding.

The human parental formula can be easily written as follows: believing parent plus good education and firm foundation equals great, perfect children. But our will and recipes are far than God's formula: hard reality plus challenging times plus basking in God's unwavering faithfulness equals an essential part of God's mission to nurture and rescue the mission of your child.

You do not own the hearts of your child. Deep inside they may be insecure and fearful, although they may not be able to admit it to themselves. They could smile on the outside but rebel as a symptom of a heart tumor that only the Lord can cure. I would wish to have the end of the tape played in our minds on God's will and purpose for our children, but we have no control but to believe the commands of Jesus to the synagogue leader: "But overhearing what they said, Jesus said to the ruler of the synagogue, 'Do not fear, only believe'" (Mark 5:35). The only remedy in times of pain, heartache, and grief is faith. Just as Jesus raised the dead girl with power of words, in the same way spiritual life is given to those who are in sin and have detoured.

Victory Assured

It bothered me why some people who turn on God ask, like the psalmist asked, "Why do the wicked prosper?" "Truly God is good to Israel, to those who are pure in heart. But as for me, my feet had almost stumbled. For I was envious of the arrogant when I saw the prosperity of the wicked (Psalm 73:1–3).

You might envy the prosperity of the wicked, but here is

a word to the wise: this is a psalm that can speak to many parents. We seek to serve God and be faithful to him. It is easy to envy others' prosperity and wonder whether serving God pays off, even in your storm. I take this challenging train ride with hope. Sometimes I wish I could undo some of the parental outcomes, but I am discouraged. I cannot be a locomotive operator and navigate this train to a perfect parental journey. But I choose to move on with a God that never fails to take me on a victorious parental journey! You will be victorious because Jesus is victorious and desires you to parent in victory.

Lifestyle

My dear friend and co laborer in the work of God, as we read and study God's Word, the Holy Spirit guides and convicts us, as in the book of Deuteronomy: "So you shall keep the commandments of the LORD your God by walking in his ways and by fearing him" (Deuteronomy 8:6). Another good scripture for your relationship with God comes from the book of Proverbs: "My son, be attentive to my words; incline your ear to my sayings. Let them not escape from your sight; keep them within your heart. For they are life to those who find them, and healing to all their flesh. Keep your heart with all vigilance, for from it flow the springs of life" (Proverbs 4:20–23). With this light, let us together unpack who this God is—his character.

The Attributes of God

God is omniscient. He knows everything possible—your parenting, all events, all creatures, and the past, present, and future. According to Daniel, "He reveals deep and hidden things; he knows what is in the darkness, and the light dwells with him" (Daniel 2:22). We can say as the psalmist, "Such knowledge is too wonderful for me; it is high, I cannot attain it" (Psalm 139:6).

You may see only a fraction of the whole picture, whereas God has the entire picture. God knows what he is doing, and he can be to do what is right according to his perfect plan over the lives of you and your wayward child. Our heavenly Father loves and listens to us even when our senses tells us he is distant. "Oh, the depth of the riches and wisdom and knowledge of God! How unsearchable are his judgments and how inscrutable his ways! For who has known the mind of the Lord, or who has been his counselor?" (Romans 11:33).

God in Partnership

Where are you, God? That is a silent question in these times of trouble. It is easy to believe God when everything goes according to our plans. But when we assume we know what a good God would do, and he does not do it our way, that is when things can get a bit complicated. It is where doubts are formed and disappointment grows. We can be tempted to distance ourselves from God with a heart of distrust. I think that is why resetting how we define good is such a big part of learning to rely on our trustworthy God.

Remarkably, God invites us to work with him as junior members in the partnership in this journey to accomplish his work in our children and day-to-day family affairs. Apostle John states, "All things were made through Him and without Him nothing was made that was made" (John 1:3). We motivate ourselves to fight to match what we script out for our children's lives, and we have a mental picture that God is good and believe it. God himself is good. Moreover, that means his plans for our children. Therefore we are right: his ways are good, and we can trust him at all times.

After I have lived for more than five decades, the experiences and my life unfolding in my eyes have left me wondering and thinking whether God makes sense according to my urges, my expectations, and my version of God's right timing, provision, and protection. In my earlier years of life, before my Damascus encounter and life-transforming encounter, I was the life of the party. Like any other teen or young adult, I had a full life ahead of me. Later, after getting married, I gave my life to Christ at age twenty-nine, and I have not looked back. I live by the faith of the Son of God. I cast myself with childlike faith and say I know whom I have believed. If we desire to believe, he becomes a close friend.

Through my parenting journey, I have had my amazing whys precipitated by uncontrollable circumstances, needing divine intervention not only by knowing but requiring action on my part: studying God's Word and prayer and fellowship with the brethren.

Facing Persecution and Fear

With about 7.6 billion people on planet Earth, are you not amazed that God knows you and each one personally. No calculator can count God's wonderful creations, including the trillions of stars and billions of galaxies in the universe, yet he knows them all by name. So is it possible that God has the blueprint of your child's life?

In suffering, there may be a tendency to get others' opinions. In my own parental challenges, someone made a comment about my job and coping in times of crisis, and I explained the impressive job title, a humble brag, to give the impression all was well despite the desperate parental pain I was in. Did I redefine myself with my job title? Were there labels associated with the season of my parental journey? Are you discouraged for the labels you currently have?

I discovered something amazing: silence is golden at times and necessary. You do not have to throw stones at every dog that barks. That's deep but true. Remind yourself of Jesus warning his disciples regarding persecution: "And do not fear those who kill the body but cannot kill the soul. Rather fear him who can destroy both soul and body in hell" (Matthew 10:28).

From a spiritual level, Jesus was not a stranger to persecution and clearly warned his disciples to be well prepared by avoiding things that gave advantage to their enemies. That way they would not be surprised but would confirm their faith and count the cost. Matthew Henry, one of my favorite Bible commentators, states that persecutors are worse than beasts by preying upon those of their own kind.

Persecution hurts and is more grievous from family, friends, and close relations in your parental pain. I am no stranger to it! King David was not a stranger to slander, which left him tearful and fearful: "All day long they injure my cause; all their thoughts are against me for evil" (Psalm 56:5).

As an ambassador of Christ, in your parent role it's best to cast the cares to God. Do well rather than speak well. When your parenting is publicly exposed with grievous, private devastation, remember you are more valuable than many sparrows. In the midst of chaos and unimaginable battles, King David prayed earnestly and honestly: "When I am afraid, I put my trust in you. In God, whose word I praise, in God I trust; I shall not be afraid. What can flesh do to me?" (Psalm 56:3–4).

Where do you turn to in times of fierce parental battles and fears? We have a model: David is a man after God's heart. Put your total trust in God for your children and family. With this awareness comes comfort, peace, counsel, and wisdom of a serpent that is as harmless as doves. Better still, you cannot journey through in your own strength—you have limited power.

True Identity

With a deeper understanding of God's Word and knowing his perfect will and purpose, life makes more sense than ever before. Before, I would question every move of my life, but with every test of my faith via trials and tribulations, I have a better understanding of my Lord. Only God gives you and your child the right name. Our identity is in Christ alone. There is no need for covering up with some comparison innuendos. Face the situation flat out and remind yourself of who you are!

God is omnipresent, unlike Satan, the enemy who has boundaries and deserves no credit at all. Our God is everywhere, including in your life and your children's life. He knows every nitty-griity detail of your past, present, and future, confirmed by Jesus in the gospel of Luke: "Why, even the hairs of your head are all numbered. Fear not; you are of more value than many sparrows" (Luke 12:7).

Be restored by the joy of salvation!

We can grow through fellowship because we are members of Christ's body. My gratitude goes to my second born sister, Margaret, a friend and a mentor who, in my baby Christian walk, introduced me to prayer and taking God at his Word through morning devotion. Back in Kenya, it was referred to as morning glory, countless lunch hour meetings, and evening prayer. "If it is not from Genesis to Revelation, it is not worth hearing" is a statement ingrained in my heart to sieve through the many voices and noises out there.

This is my testimony of taking God at his Word, believing him, and experiencing his goodness and mercy. Living side by side with my family, faithful friends, and faith family has exponentially led to my spiritual growth through fellowship. Despite the challenges and circumstances I faced, I was able to live to God's full potential and embrace life with the joy of the Lord. I often attended home group cells and Bible study home fellowships, looking pretty and smiling but bleeding on the inside, with scars and emotional wounds. I listened to other parents' testimonies and life issues, and I realized that only God knows our hearts. Deep inside, people may be insecure and fearful. I realized God wants us to become a body of believers doing life together, which the Greek call *koinonia*, a fellowship and communion with fellow Christians.

I remember having fellowship at our home one Thursday evening. A sister in Christ shared an incident concerning her son being charged with a felony due to possession of a group three controlled substance, and she requested prayers to fight the charges and obtain a more favorable outcome. I was so glad I did not give up the meeting that day despite my busy schedule, with a deadline to submit my thesis before midnight. The sister's prayer request, the fellowship worship, and the sharing of the Word were used to encourage and strengthen me. Many more have been used to grow my faith, and God has used me to help others. The Scriptures shared could not be more transparent, and knowing him and his promises made more sense.

Living Side by Side

In one of the reflections on life together, one of our pastors invited the congregation to consider how God creates and sustains faith in our hearts through his Word, spoken to us by our fellow brothers and sisters in Christ. One of my favorite quotes on fellowship of believers is, "To be God's people is to be the people who hear God's Word and speak it to one another."

Are you seeking to serve God's plan and trust him in your parental journey? Maybe you are emotionally drained and discouraged to see your child struggling. Are you compelled by the need to show the world you have a "perfect family" according to societal norms instead of committing to what God wants you to do? Psalm 37:5 is clear: "Commit your ways to the Lord, trust in Him, and he will act."

As a post–COVID-19 patient, I have learned I am still a work in process. I believe that though I only see and imagine the piece of the puzzle, God has the whole mystery. He can be trusted to do what he has promised according to his perfect plan. When I was on the verge of death from the deadly virus, I had no choice but to trust him at his Word for healing, and he miraculously did it. Glory be to his name! Why not trust him with my children's plans and future? He changes not.

I recently embarked on preventative and curative care with this virus. One incident caught my attention: the growing list of strange coronavirus symptoms. As the pandemic rigorously spreads with many unanswered questions, it is a clear indication that our humanity, our fleshly being, has limitations. With limited scientific facts and evidence, there is need for answers. It only makes sense to live by faith and not figure out each circumstance in your life, relying on your feelings and emotions. Your flesh will fail you, and you cannot depend on it to lead or assess your parental world. Apply the truths of God's Word in parenting.

Run the Race: A Poem for Parents in Pain

Take it to the Lord.
God is not so unkind.
Dealing with unselfishness, saving us unto ourselves.
Wait upon the Lord.
This God has done something. Showing
kindness, God leads to repentance.
Learning to see the events are
Focused on the good news and the person of
his Son, Jesus, his triumph returned.
All our hearts break; confusion will be brought.
Be still and know he is God.
Furthermore, have emotional wholeness.

The Supernatural Nature of God

During my time in isolation and quarantine from COVID-19, in my search for preventative and curative measures to beat the monster disease, I came across the use and benefits of coconut water. Coconut water is naturally hydrating and replenishes electrolytes after work, fitness, and other daily activities, as per the advertisement.

My hubby and I got into discussing the coconut and how water is mysteriously found in the coconut. Mostly they are found on the coast of Kenya, where he lived before he met his wife to be—yes, me! I lived in central part of the country, where coconuts were a rare commodity, though they were well celebrated when found and used in many recipes.

In Kenya, most coconut trees are found in the coastal counties. A coastal highland county also has a small population of coconut trees, and the area under production is continually increasing.

Evidence-based research from WebMD shows coconut water super hydrates with many health benefits. It is a sweet, translucent fluid that you may drink straight from young green coconuts. Coconut water formation can be a hard concept to grasp at first. The water comes naturally from within the fruit and is referred to as the liquid endosperm. As the young coconut matures, the coconut water starts to harden to form coconut meat, known as the solid.

As our conversation about the water formation in coconuts progressed, our teenage daughter joined the chat. The conversation became complex and exciting, and she googled for a better explanation, almost leading to the next trending thing on social media.

The complex formation of water in a coconut illustrates our limitation in our perception of things that the mind can only imagine. It is not as easy as X, Y, and Z, but an in-depth study can be comprehended by a fifteen-year-old and create some workable solutions.

As followers of Jesus Christ, our human minds cannot explain away the supernatural nature of God. Don't we try to fix the puzzle with arguments and scientific evidence of a silent God? Our minds, intellect, and feelings fail us most times and make no sense when we try to reason. It sets us in unfathomable pain and unbelief, and sometimes we are mental wrecks. God works in mysterious ways, His ways are not our ways, and he loves us even when we cannot understand.

Bereavement

In my family, I lost my loving sister Kinjo, my loving mom, my loving brother George, and my dad in a span of a few years. In every incident, I struggled with emotional pain and did not feel God's presence, and there was no good reason. I worked the severe "Why the tragedies?" lamentation.

In one incident, after my mother's death, to say my tears that rolled my cheeks would fill an eight-ounce mug is an understatement. The throbbing emotional heartache and wounds were so deep and left me emotionally paralyzed. I thought it was a bad dream, but it was a reality that I get to live today! Why the gap? Emotions are flawed, contradicting the very beliefs in God to characterize my daily work.

> For the eyes of the Lord are over the righteous, and his ears are open to their prayers. But the face of the Lord is against those who do evil. (1 Peter 3:12)

My plea and instincts were longing for that perfect child, that perfect family, that perfection that is knitted in the very heart of our souls. We do not live in that "perfect" world. But was I wrong to express and act in my own emotions and will? Maybe not. Satan thrives in those dull moments of disillusionment to kill your joy and steal it, and finally it leads to a road of destruction, depression, mental anguish, and family chaos

A trained biblical counselor should know better, right ? But who takes care of the caregivers when their tanks are running on empty, but everyone assumes they are healthy and courageous? We know even the brightest thing can become dull, and only God knows our innermost thoughts. Isaiah 55:8–9 states, "'For My thoughts are not your thoughts, Neither are your ways My ways,' declares the Lord. 'For as the heavens are higher than the earth, So are My ways higher than your ways, And My thoughts than your thoughts.'"

Fruitful Growth in the Faith through Tragedy and Family Bereavement

In my more than five decades of life, I have worn many hats, including teacher, hospice crisis care nurse, and biblical counselor. Becoming a biblical counselor came from a need to understand God and come to the knowledge of his Word according to in-depth study. It was an eye-opener and gave me the fulfillment of parenting that "I may know Him and the power of His resurrection and the Fellowship of His sufferings being conformed to His death" (Philippians 3:10). We are planted in a stream in the midst of an arid land, and we are the tree and the stream. Let's get serious and pursue God in our journey. Blessed are those who seek God, for they will find God and bear fruit with a permanent significance. God's holy Word transforms us day and night. Meditation of his Word squeezes the disappointment out! He knows the way of the righteous, and it is a blessed life. The road is narrow, but it is worth it. It is the path of blessing!

Praise and Worship God

Cultivating a heart of praise and worship played a significant role in healing, singing, and reciting the goodness of God for the gift of the womb. My loving husband, Bob, and my exceptional children have unique talents.

> Open my eyes, that I may behold wondrous things
> out of your law.
> I am a sojourner on the earth: hide not your
> commandments from me!
> My soul is consumed with longing for your rules!
> (Psalm 119:18–20)

We are bringing wholeness to the heart and sanity to the mind. We are thinking of God as he is lapsed into wonder, connecting with prayer, cultivating a spirit of surrender, and making ourselves small in submitting to God's will to parent better. The Lord is our shepherd, and the sheep are entirely dependent on the shepherd. This is essential for peace amid the parental storm. We shall unpack the power of prayer in the next chapters.

Learn to Pause

Do you ever feel anxious or depressed in the face of circumstances that feel entirely out of your control? Me too! A verse that has been a great source of comfort to me in those times has been Lamentations 3:24, "'The Lord is my portion,' says my soul, therefore I will hope in him."

"Wait for" means pause. Hit the pause button and do not react to everything around you—the child's whisper, the cry, the fear, and the unknown! Some therapy does not harm in those dull moments. Taking deep breaths, calling to mind scriptures, and preaching to oneself out loud does help.

You can feel out of control, but do not act out of control, because you remember who is in control. He is your portion, and therefore you will wait for him.

Not Ashamed, and Rightly Dividing the Word of Truth

I did most of my internship and service for my biblical counseling studies at Our Faith Family Church at Bear Creek. The most fulfilling and spiritual nourishment was on Wednesday night at AWANA. AWANA stands for Approved Workmen Are Not Ashamed, and it is taken from 2 Timothy 2:15, "Do your best to present yourself to God as one approved, a worker who has no need to be ashamed, rightly handling the word of truth." Seeing the children recite this verse from heart challenged me to hide God's Word in my heart—and better still, rightly divide the Word of truth. You have to like the heart of a child!

God promised a keeper against odds when it looked hopeless. Abraham believed the promise and expected God to fulfill it. He took God at his Word, and as a result he became the father of many nations. God's declaration over him came to pass:

"In hope, he believed against hope, that he should become the father of many nations, as he had been told, 'So shall your offspring be'" (Romans 4:18). When God makes a promise, what do we do with it? Does he have the power to bring it to pass even when all the evidence and surrounding circumstances run contrary to what he said? Abraham's hope was in God, not humans, time, events, or his physical being. God makes a promise, and it contains the self-fulfilling power to bring it to pass. Isaiah states, "So shall my word be that goes out from my mouth; it shall not return to me empty, but it shall accomplish that which I purpose, and shall succeed in the thing for which I sent it (Isaiah 55:11).

Abraham was steadfast and did not allow people's opinions to influence him. Who is affecting you? You too can purposely walk by faith and overcome the parenting challenges around you. When you feel hopeless to return to his Word, he has never failed to fulfill it. Every promise about your child is possible. Draw on your faith, his unfailing love, and prayer.

Dr. David Jeremiah states in his book *Shelter in God*, "What I do know is what He has done! And that is what we can count on. The God who sheltered His people in biblical days will not stop now. So, come what may, I am trusting in the sheltering God to be my refuge. And so can you."

He has done for others, including respecters of no persons. He will do it for your child. "You have been a refuge to the poor, a shelter for the needy in their distress, a refuge from the storm and a shade from the heat" (Isaiah 25:4).

Turbulence

To me, 2019 is an unforgettable year, but it is not worse than the COVID-19 experience of the year 2020, discussed in previous chapters. After a jubilant Christmas with family on way back to work, the pilot did not mince words to say there was turbulence expected on the flight, and lo and behold, the announcement of severe turbulence caused silence on the plane. There was not much to do but trust on the captain to navigate the plane to the best of his expertise. I recall praying in my mother tongue, "But God saw us through." "But I will have mercy on the house of Judah, and I will save them by the LORD their God"(Hosea 1:7a).

Sometimes our parental journeys may hit turbulence, where we can trust only the captain of our lives to navigate through the storms. These are the challenging and painful situations where we develop teachable hearts and are assured of a safe landing, a harvest of righteousness. Do you realize that after a miracle or great time of ministry, Jesus was faced with trials and storms? In turbulent times, we learn how God brings about parental pruning in a spiritual process to make our lives fruitful. But who is ready for the pruning? Who sees the storm coming? Are we prepared for the pruning? What is the Father doing when we enter a parental pruning season?

My home church pastor, David Welch at Bear Creek Baptist Church, has been there for more than a decade, with thousands of inspiring and transformative messages about the gospel. He once preached a message that resonates with me today in my parental journey on pruning.

> He prunes you to cut away sin.
> He prunes you to form Christ's character in you.
> He prunes you to make me a more assertive parent.
> He prunes you to produce something unexpected for His glory.
> How is God pruning you during this parenting season?

Living in His Presence

What do you do when you do not know what to do? Worship is an understatement in times of uncertainty. As the songwriter Helen H. Lemmel sang, "Turn your eyes upon Jesus, Look full in His wonderful face, and the things of earth will grow strangely dim, in the light of His glory and grace."

Call on His Name

There are times when you do not know what to say, but the beautiful name of Jesus has power, just as Ruth C. Jones wrote in the hymn "The Solid Rock."

> In times like this, you need a Savior
> In times like this, you need an anchor Be very sure, be very sure,
> Your anchor is the Solid Rock.
> This Rock is Jesus. Yes, He is the one.

There is just something about that name. Jesus! Jesus! Jesus! Jesus. He is everywhere! He carried you through! He is always within us; at times when you feel down-hearted.

God Specializes in Pop Quizzes

One of my instructors in my nursing school specialized in pop quizzes, which required a high grade to pass the class. Passing a pop quiz depends on how well you are prepared. This called for burning the midnight oil, studying, and graduating to start providing for the family! Failure was not an option, and I was grateful to have my name ingrained in that school of nursing as the best student of the year. Nevertheless, I take pride for a higher purpose. My name is written and rooted in the book of life after a successful journey, looking to hear the Master say, "Well done, faithful tool formed into a human soul. You represented me well as an ambassador, obeying my promises and methods to parents, even in detours!"

Jesus Is Our Perfect Hope

When God calls us his vessel in his hands, he takes us on a mission to accomplish, even if our hearts are bloody and oozing with mental and emotional pain.

That in our minds keeps our spiritual gauges on full!

Every true Christ believer will trust God's purpose without knowing why,

Even in the senseless contradictions that we face in our lives.

Trusting God's purpose even when facing trials and nothing makes no sense,

To believe in the fruit of the womb then.

You may be silently battling in your mind, saying, "It makes no sense to the belief that my child will be the head and not the tail."

And then fall into the devil's trap, and he takes you on guilt trip of thoughts: my daughter is homeless, my child is a prostitute, my daughter is barren. These are not foreign concepts from Bible stories. See a mockery from Peninahs.

Are you mocked, teased or rejected due to your child's detours? Hannah is no stranger, as stated in 1 Samuel 1:6–16.

> Peninnah teased Hannah to make her angry. She did it because the LORD had kept Hannah from having children. Peninnah teased Hannah year after year. Every time Hannah would go up to the house of the Lord, Elkanah's other wife would tease her. She would keep doing it until Hannah cried and wouldn't eat. Her husband Elkanah would speak to her. He would say, "Hannah, why are you crying? Why don't you eat? Why are you so angry and unhappy? Don't I mean more to you than ten sons?" One time when they had finished eating and drinking in Shiloh, Hannah stood up. The priest Eli was sitting on a chair by the doorpost of the LORD's house. Hannah was very bitter. She sobbed and sobbed. She prayed to the Lord. She made a promise to him. She said, "Lord, you rule over all. Please see how I'm suffering! Show concern for me! Don't forget about me! Please give me a son! If you do, I'll give him back to you. Then he will serve you all the days of his life. He'll never use a razor on his head. He'll never cut his hair." As Hannah kept on praying to the Lord, Eli watched her lips. She was praying in her heart. Her lips were moving. But she wasn't making a sound. Eli thought Hannah was drunk. He said to her, "How long will you keep on getting drunk? Get rid of your wine." "That's not true, sir," Hannah replied. "I'm a woman who is deeply troubled. I haven't been drinking wine or beer. I was telling the LORD all of my troubles. Don't think of me as an evil woman. I've been praying here because I'm very sad. My pain is so great."

All I know is you have a covenant with God. He is a covenant-keeping God! And He remembered Hannah and blessed her with the fruit of the womb, who became the first of the prophets after Moses and the last Judge of Israel!

God is a promise keeper who changes not. Whatever you are crying for in pain, lay it down because what He has for you is far better than what your eyes have seen or your ears have heard, and it is better than your feelings!

Expect a miracle even when you don't understand the whys.
God continues to work in you and through you as a parent.
The eyes of the heavenly father are upon you!
The good news is it is not even your battle but the Lord's.
You are worried about it, sleepless nights.
Quit the defeated attitude.
The enemy is out to destroy you.
Joseph would have said, Wake me up when it is over.
Your help is available.
Moses, with children of Israel, would say the Lord shall fight for you if you hold your peace.
Hold your peace!
The Lord will fight for you.
For your good and his glory!

God Is Sovereign

Job faced unfathomable pain, but in the end, Job's faith was more significant, and his health was more excellent. Amid the storm, Job lost sight of God's presence. Job 23:8–9 says, "Behold, I go forward, but he is not there, and backward, but I do not perceive him; on the left hand when he is working, I do not behold him; he turns to the right hand, but I do not see him." However, Job resolved to keep his faith in God and stated, "But He knows the way that I take; when he has tested me. I will come out as gold" (Job 23:10). This is an excellent example of how to live by faith and not by sight. The circumstances and situations in our children's lives may not be to your expectation, but it is in those challenging seasons of parenting days when our feelings and events do not make sense that decisions of unwavering faith are demanded.

Amid a child's trials, there will be times you do not feel the presence of the Lord but choose by the power of the Holy Spirit to be still. Pray and search God. Listen and reason with him in your war room.

Moreover, when the battle gets intense, I am not sure about you, but I ask for more ammunition and backup from sisters of grace. A reminder of Aaron and Hur, who supported Moses in the war with the Amalekites when his hands grew tired. They took a stone and put it under Moses to sit on while they held Moses's hand so that Israel could prevail. Who is holding your arms?

Without trials and suffering, we would be hopeless. Part of experiencing the fullness of our children's destinies and our calling as parents is understanding the detours. Our character would not be straightened, nor our faith is strengthened. As Apostle Peter stated, "You rejoice in this, though now for a short time you have had to struggle in various trials so that the genuineness of your Faith—more valuable than gold, which perishes though refined by fire—may result in praise, glory, and honor at the revelation of Jesus Christ" (1 Peter 1:6–7).

Part of understanding and finding meaning in our lives is derived from a sense of belonging, accomplishments, purpose, and storytelling. Yet such foundations are not strong enough to give us a meaningful life; it was never about the meaning we make but the sense that made us with a transforming knowledge of the living God.

Parenting That Works!

We all aspire to raise children who turn out well and desire to raise children who turn out great, right? Good intentions are not good enough. Parents, our best purpose can fail, so having a spiritual dissection is essential! I read an interesting piece from an Indian journal. Using reason without applying it to experience leads only to theoretical illusions. Ideas derived from real-world experiences lead to knowledge acquisition, and the accumulation of time-tested principles leads to wisdom. The same guide with the Bible and application, particularly parenting, lets our heavenly Father mold us and our children as vessels and tools in our Father's hands, with his God-given resources, the gift and fruit of the Spirit.

Far too often as parents, we fail to understand the detours in our children's lives and view them wrongly. We give in to anger and bitterness and sometimes miss the growth that comes with it. Are we too hard on ourselves? Are there detours that can be ignored? Luke, one of the twelve disciples of Jesus Christ, wrote in the book of Acts, "And the times of this ignorance God winked at; but now commandeth all men everywhere to repent" (Acts 17:30).

Parent, what is your purpose?

My son Derrick shared with me his experience, and the most important lesson at a Christian leadership program was finding one's purpose. I gladly ask the same question to us and stand on Romans 8:28a, "All things work together for your good for those who love God." This is not a cliché. It is the unchanging Word. As a parent, you are bleeding on the inside, feeling helpless and ashamed, with nowhere to bury your head because of the shame surrounding you. You want a quick fix, God's edition of your child, and a repaired heart. How about you take God at his word, set your sight on him, bask in his promises, and let him bathe you in his glory? Let God be God in your parenting journey, and create an atmosphere of grace. We will discuss the storms we face as parents and how God works in those senseless situations.

Unless we live in his presence each day, needing him every minute, we may think we know how to parent the best way possible, and it is a joy to know God is in the business of restoration regarding our children, home, family, friends, and hurting relationships. The Lord will help us during times of difficulty to set our faith in him even when our sight tells us otherwise and makes no sense. As James 1:12–13 states, "Blessed is the man who remains steadfast under trial, for when he has stood the test, he will receive the crown of life, which God has promised to those who love him ... Afterward, they will receive the crown of life that God has promised to those who love him."

No Earwax

Don't you love the holistic fulfillment in the Bible?

My late grandmother, who was 106 years old until she rested in eternity in September 2020, had a favorite saying from Isaiah 59:1, "Behold, the Lord's hand is not shortened, that it cannot save, or his ear dull, that it cannot hear." I reflected on his scripture and asked myself, "The Lord's hand not shortened?" I believe God's power is never lessened by our circumstances and can reach as far as the hand can. It is parallel to what God said to Moses in the book of Numbers: "And the LORD said to Moses, 'Is the LORD's hand shortened? Now you shall see whether my word will come true for you or not'" (Numbers 11:23). My adjective to describe God's mighty power is indescribable, and neither strength of the enemy nor the deep wounds of our detours can shorten the hand of almighty God. Yes, Grandma had her spiritual secret weapon!

God does not work on our schedule, but he hears and gives you and your child everything for the season. I am still discovering him daily, settling in my heart to understand the no and yes timing, aligning my will to his perfect choice.

Why were Gigs and others afflicted? Why did Wayne die at her prime age, leaving behind a son who has numerous unanswered questions? Those who judged you and in ways used your season of parental pain to mock and reject you say,

"I do not know what I would if that was my child." This hurts profoundly and makes no sense.

How do you live out an extraordinary parenting journey when experiencing detours in your child's life? With the knowledge of God's attributes, we have the answers.

God is divine. His ways are not man's ways. He cannot be compared with any other god. Why? Because he guides my adventures because he is an eagle God.

Through his mighty power, which is like a rushing wind, he carries me to my destiny without sweat on my part. His only begotten Son, Jesus Christ, is your pacesetter, and he has promised you more incredible things than those he did here on Earth. We are joined to him through salvation, and therefore we reign with him now and forever.

The heart of the *matter is in* Psalm 23:4, "Even though I walk through the valley of the shadow of death, I shall fear no evil ... for thou art with me."

I learned that I have always failed miserably the many times I have been dependent on myself during my parental journey. I end up wasting both my energy and time. As a sheep, I have also learned that I need a shepherd; otherwise, I might lead myself into a slaughterhouse. I can now sing the song by Robert Critchley: *"My hope is built on nothing less than Jesus's blood and Righteousness."* That is why I can testify boldly that through God's divine presence, I will go where he leads me and do what he tells me to do, for if God is on my side, who can be against me?" (Romans 8:31). His divine presence will clear every barrier, and even during this period of lockdown, my destiny is not locked.

Sovereign God

Prophet Isaiah directs us to make best use of our senses, give deep thought to creation, give thanks to God, and glorify Him for His sovereignty.

> Lift your eyes and look to the heavens: Who created all these?
> He who brings out the starry host one by one and calls forth each of them by name.
> Because of his great power and mighty strength, not one of them is missing.
> Why do you complain, Jacob? Why do you say, Israel, "My way is hidden from the Lord; my cause is disregarded by my God"? Do you not know? Have you not heard?
> The Lord is the everlasting God, the Creator of the ends of the earth. He will not grow tired or weary and his understanding no one can fathom. He gives strength to the weary and increases the power of the weak. Even youths grow tired and weary, and young men stumble and fall; Thirty-one but those who hope in the Lord will renew their strength. They will soar on wings like eagles; they will run and not grow weary, and they will walk and not be faint. (Isaiah 40:26–31)

Although applicable to parenting all children, this book is primarily focused on equipping parents who are raising children who have experienced significant trauma or loss in the early years of life, unexpected transitions, detours, loss of a child, or extensive medical care for a child. It is for those who feel like God is silent.

Understanding your ambassadorial calling derives your resources from the highest God and showers you with his infinite power, presence, wisdom, and grace. As a faithful Father, God can parent you in return to accord the same for your children.

I leave you with the words of one of my favorite authors, Tripp, from his book *Parenting*, states, "Parenting is about the willingness to live a life of long-term, intentional repetition, God has called you to a life of patient perseverance. He has called you to be willing to do the same thing over and over again. He has called you to look for opportunities every day to be part of his process of grace in the lives of your children. He has called you to be His tool of grace again and again and again. Parenting really is a life of holy repetition. Tripp, Paul; *"Parenting"*(Wheaton Illinois: Crossway 2016),page 208.

4

Stand Out In Fit-In Generation

What we see of the creature should lead us to the Creator.

—Matthew Henry

On a hot Thursday afternoon, my teen daughter got home from school and shouted, "Mom, guess what? Today the best that happened was a message from a guest speaker from the Fellowship of Christian Athletes(FCA). She said we need to live by the understanding that we were meant to stand out, not fit in!"

That was deep, and I said to myself, "I need it more than my teen daughter!"

It is probably one of our best mother-daughter moments that resonates with me in our daily discussion of the good, bad, and ugly. It is an outlet to let out bottled-up emotions or simply have giggle moments.

The Real Dilemma for Parents

Do children come out with a clean slate for parents to write on? If parents do their part, then the results will be brilliant, self-reliant, and adjusted for the child. Anything contrary to that is a parental failure!

I was brought up by a former police officer and businessman, and the tone of voice would be considered harsh from a layman, but it is a command in military terms. The care and confidence my father exhibited were nondebatable and nonnegotiable. No matter the storm in life, they stood to the occasion.

Today, our children need to see more confidence from our parents, less unconscious, and less guilt, therefore drawing a balance of certainty and vulnerability.

Where do we draw a line between bad relationships that corrupt good morals with inadequate parenting? Do children come up with a manuscript or instructions? I am the wrong person to answer this question.

Who takes the credit when our children turn out well or badly? Who is to blame? Does good parenting produce good children, and vice versa? Common sense says to look for the easy answer and ambiguous assurance. Some people will make decisions based on cultural influences and genetic mechanisms. Other factors assume that a wayward child is a total sum of his feelings and real choices. He has a will; he chooses and pursues a path that he has selected. I echo the words of Paul from Romans 7:24, "What a wretched man I am! Who will deliver me from this body of death?" Several factors affect a child's capacity to make certain choices: genes, environmental factors at home, social environment, and school. But even with the best intentions, many parents are haunted by a sense of failure! The blame game has no substance, but getting to the chore of the issue and addressing it alleviates the problem. How many of us take the choices seen as sin and address them from that perspective?

Successful Child versus Parental Identity

What will I blame it on? Or do my thoughts deceive me regarding what I consider a successful person? "The best thing you will ever inherit from me is education," is a statement I heard over and over while growing up. Could it have shaped my irrational thinking and action upon a successful future? The expectation and demand for academic excellence, the running from one extra activity to another, a weekend filled with trips, tournaments, museums, and community—it all projects significant commitments. Still, it can lead to emotional, mental, and physical exhaustion in children and parents!

I am not sure about you, but I needed a reexamination of my belief system. More so, when one of my children did not pursue the Reserve Officer Training Corps (ROTC) and tennis, I was disappointed in the sense of their accomplishments and my expectations for them. Could it be my identity and purpose? Could it have been fulfilled in my children's achievement? In all honesty, it led to my anger and frustration. In addition, my lack of self-control was justified due to their desires and endeavors. These are teachable moments in the parenting journey.

Parents, we need to look for our identity in Christ and not in our children. Otherwise, we would be chasing the wind. Peter the Apostle explains it better: "For this very reason, make every effort to supplement your faith with virtue, and virtue with knowledge, and to knowledge self-control; and self-control, with steadfastness; and steadfastness with godliness; and godliness, brotherly affection; and to brotherly affection with love. For if these qualities are yours and are increasing, they will keep you from being ineffective and unfruitful in your knowledge of our Lord Jesus Christ. For whoever lacks these qualities is so nearsighted that he is blind, having forgotten that he was cleansed from his former sin" (2 Peter 1:5–9).

Grace-based Parent

Parents may ask, "How can I rear my children to be successful?" It is an open-ended question, and instead I suggest asking, "How can I be a grace-based parent?"

This point reflects and points to a pathway to successful parenting, results, and what a parent can do to cope. The lack of grace has led me to reflect on my shortcomings, weaknesses, impatience, immaturity, resentment, weariness, and anxieties. As Peter states regarding confirming one's calling and election, "His divine power has given us everything we need for a godly life through our knowledge of him who called us by his glory and goodness. Through these, he has given us his very great and precious promises so that through them you may participate in the divine nature, having escaped the corruption in the world caused by evil desires" (Peter 1:3–4). Martin Luther said, "The Bible is the cradle wherein Christ is laid." Read it!

Emerging Theories

In the nineteenth century, the emergence of behavioral science came to the child's rescue, highlighting behavioral patterns in children with a scientific explanation such as drinking, rebellion, temper tantrums, lying, stealing, masturbation, and adolescent turmoil, to name a few associated with faulty parenting. Was this a tree of good and evil in a parental garden that was into a cold and hostile world? The tradition was constant, but the scientific theories are static, and to our surprise you realize your theory of parenting was wrong, and all you did was detrimental to the child. But how about the emerging theories?

Let's take the example of "A chip off the old block." It's an informal way to say someone is very similar in character to a parent. They were describing people with the same qualities. A meeting of minds idiom: son and father, or mother and a daughter. They usually had negative connotations when reference the father, or implied being a prostitute if referring to the mother. In the old days, they would give the warning and get away with it.

Parents, God Is Your Comforter

The Word of God gives you a calming sense of your life and your emotions. When a parent hurts, Isaiah states, "As one whom his mother comforts, so will I comfort you: You shall be comforted in Jerusalem" (Isaiah 66:13). On the battlefield of life, Christians have been assured victory. How? Jesus told the disciples, "I am with you" (Isaiah 41:10).

Jesus, the defeater of death, our Savior, is with you and me in the battle. Jesus is our secret weapon. Let's fight from victory, not for victory. "He has walked joyfully with others and so he can because the book of Hebrews reminds Jesus Christ is the same yesterday, today, and forever" *Hebrews 13:8).

The power of the gospel can radically transform. The psalmist states, "Those who trust in the LORD are like Mount Zion, which cannot be shaken but endures forever. As the mountains surround Jerusalem, so the LORD surrounds his people both now and forevermore" (Psalm 125:1).

Legitimate Concern versus Illegitimate Worry

God allows for genuine, legitimate concern, but when you constantly worry, you have crossed over to the other side and given Satan a field day in your parenting life and family. There is a temptation and tendency to turn legitimate concern to illegitimate worry. We need to be responsibly concerned because the situation is real.

Are you trying to figure out all things and the feeling of what will happen to your child? The legitimate concern is of the situation, but was the worry illegitimate? Do you ask,

"What's going on with my child, and how do I make it through?" The shame, the anger, the bitterness, are a fleshly human response that should not take precedence in a believer's life. The journey takes twists and turns and affects our lives and families. Parents are concerned because a child's dream has been cut off, as well as the shame this brought to the family. But illegitimate worry is when worry is controlling you, but you are not controlling the situation and how you respond to it. Worry tells you that you can't sleep now. Worry starts to dictate your well-being. You have crossed over from legitimate, responsible concern to illegitimate action. Yes, God allows for legitimate, responsible concern, but not worry.

From scripture, we know so well Jesus warns us about our thoughtfulness of this world. Instead, we should divert our efforts and care to our souls, which has eternal value as evidenced in the gospel of Matthew: "And which of you by being anxious can add a single hour to his span of life?" (Matthew 6:27).

God Is Our Father!

God wants us to call our shots and to submit to him and his authority as parents. He is a loving Father. Jesus, from His teaching on prayer, reveals God as Father, in the gospel of Matthew: "Our Father in heaven, hallowed be your name" (Matthew 6:9). We start this prayer by professing our core belief that God is our heavenly Father, the all-knowing and all-powerful one. Jesus repeatedly said, "Don't worry," because you have a Father, if only you can think of God as a Father in the midst of this chaos where nothing makes sense. As earlier stated, he is immutable, sovereign, powerful, and above all else a daddy! Yes, there is a difference between a father and a daddy. He is a daddy with a sense of relief. Take a deep breath. That's the sense of his care in the middle of a parenting crisis, when he does not make sense from our perspective and circumstances.

The sense of a father, and better yet a daddy, brings down a calming sense in your emotions, and the parenting journey makes sense.

In Matthew, Jesus makes a convincing statement. There is the story of Jesus walking on the water toward his fearful disciples in the midst of the storm. "And he asked his disciples 'Why are you afraid, O you of little faith?' Then he rose and rebuked the winds and the sea, and there was a great calm" (Matthew 8:26). The situation was frightening, a reason of concern, with the angry waves hitting a reeling boat.

Crisis has a way of creating something good or bad. It creates more caring siblings, families, and relationships. It strengthens the family and the community. But sometimes things can get shaky. There are reported cases of crisis turning into stress, which has a ripple effect on a person's health. But through the convicting scripture, God said to look into the spiritual in the midst of the medical and the physical. "The Lord passed before him and proclaimed, The Lord, the Lord a God merciful and gracious, slow to anger, and abounding in steadfast love and faithfulness" (Exodus 34:6).

The stormy trials and detours of our children come to our parenting journey quickly and hit us so profoundly that we are left reeling. Our hearts are crushed under the pressure, and we are left with tears and cries of anguish.

But the good news is Jesus went to his disciples not when the skies were blue and waves were calm, but during the storm. He went during the detours! When all hope seemed lost and disaster unavoidable, Jesus's hopeful words were, "Take heart; it is I. Do not be afraid" (Matthew 14:27). In the same manner, on the battleground of stormy ground, I say to you, Take heart!

Working for Your Good and His Glory

The answered questions make everything senseless from a human perspective, but thank God for his Spirit, conviction, and guidance. In his letter to the Romans, Paul stated, "And we know that for those who love God all things work together for good, for those who are the called according to His purpose" (Romans 8:28).

Lessons and the good learned means getting out of your comfort zone and creating family cohesion. The absence of crisis makes you pretty independent when nothing is wrong. To make sense out of parenting, have the courage to talk to a trusted faith family. Get the courage to seek help! A crisis is an opportunity for caring.

In Lack and in Plenty

"Blessed by the best" is one of my son's favorite saying. They may be said of you as a parent. Blessed with the fruit of the womb, trained, excelling in school, with the "normal" problems and challenges pulling through, and now a "success."

Your faith in Christ is helping you live responsibly and enjoy the fruits of your labor. Your income is up, your family is stable, the church is doing well, and relationships are thriving, so what else do you need as a parent? James's book was written to people who were prospering as a result of their faith, not unlike many Christians today. The gospel had brought a "social lift" to their lives, bettering their material circumstances. "But what about when calamity strikes? Trials and tribulations? Does success change the way one looks at trouble? What about the gospel—is it really necessary to take the scriptures so seriously when things are going so well? I was comfortable in my faith, but was it fruitful? Was Christ affecting more than my lifestyle?"

As he is to you, so must you be to your child. The yelling, the shouting, the anger—all are against the basic rules of parenting. Blame it on the upbringing of a strict parent? Not really, because you are a new creature in Christ Jesus, and as he is, so are you in this world, not picking and choosing but inclusive of your homeworld.

This conviction could not have come at a better time in the lowest moments, in the valley of parenting—yes, almost a shadow of death. In my duties as a crisis care hospice nurse, watching a mother or father wailing over a dying child from the effects of choices and detours at the death bed, all that mattered most was just one more hug, one more breath. "Can you open your eyes? We love you, George. Till we see you again. Please forgive me for any wrongs and heartaches I caused you as a mother." These words came from a grieving mother to a dying young adult due to throat cancer. They were like a bulb lit in my heart to awaken the truth that as God is to me, so must I be to my child. However, the still voices of the devil never cease. "This does not make sense." A road trip of anger, bitterness, and reminiscing becomes the order of the day.

There are too many questions and justification from a migrant parent. The one-sided talk or lectures may sometimes sound as follows: "I invested all my time to take you to the best schools, and I migrated to a foreign land to get you a better opportunity. You never lacked and can be counted among the privileged. I opened doors to prestigious colleges—just for you to take a detour and bring me a grandchild in your final year. What a shame!" As with all good parental reflections, the content asked an eye-opener to dormant dreams or deterred vision.

This is not dealing with a child the way the Lord has dealt with you! God has called you and me out of darkness to his marvelous light, and he deals with us parents in loving and graceful ways. His kindness, great patience, forbearing, and intolerance of sin command us to model to the child when we stand in place of God. Are sin, consequences, and discipline not part of the journey? I am glad you asked! Let's follow that thread as the journey unfolds.

Wise Counsel

For some time, I struggled with the ownership mentality of parenting. Whom can I blame it on? Upbringing? My wrong perspective? With all the responsibilities, a parent loses the bigger picture, gets confused, and opens the door for a dysfunctional family. Yielding to God's more significant and wise counsel is the only solution, Christian parents! Read carefully the list of instructions accompanying the following passages.

> But the one who looks into the perfect law, the law of liberty and perseveres, being no hearer who forgets but a doer who acts, he will be blessed in his doing. (James 1:25)
>
> These things I command you, so that you will love one another. (John 15:7)
>
> This promise is true to those who hear it and obey it. It is through the spoken word that everything came into being. (Hebrews 11:3)
>
> By faith, we understand that the ages were prepared by the word of God so that what is seen has not been made out of things which are visible. (Hebrews 11:3)

Problems That Parents Have versus Crisis

Why are you late for school? Why is your room like a hurricane? What happened to "eat your vegetables"? Aren't these problems and questions for average functional families? There are real crises, such as life-threatening illness and mental anguish to both child and parents. Children need hard work, discipline, teaching, and preparation for the future—accompanied by love. As Proverbs 16:9 states, "The heart of man plans his way, but the Lord establishes his steps." Realize the desire and joy of every parent, as noted by the following statement.

A strong, young, melanin, beautifully and wonderfully made daughter or son is resilient, tough, and unshakable. This warrior made the best out of a bad situation, and nothing can hold her or him down. The child finds the humor in anything, is optimistic, makes a dollar out of fifteen cents, and is superhuman, fierce, and bold. The child pushes and works hard at school and at summer jobs to help with the bills, relieving parents from facing foreclosure due to lost income from COVID-19. The child is the epitome an inside and outward beauty.

Heartbreaks

A mother yells at her daughter. "Over the last few months, I noticed you got angry quickly. You did not hang out with your friend Mary and wanted nothing to do with God. Instead of fellowship, you took up another job. Despite that, you have demanding assignments from your nursing degree."

The subject exacerbated the daughter's anger. "Mom, I'm okay. I will be all right."

All the above is still essential, but it could have been weighty on you, my daughter. The weight of it can be a lot. We do not talk about the burden that comes with relationships, frustrations, and trying to fit in. All of those who are faithful truly did not see this coming. Little did I know the time you bought so many over-the-counter drugs and had "a plan."

Mary was my beautiful, brilliant baby girl who was found lifeless with a note beside her bed. The investigators painfully said a word I hate to hear: it was indeed a suicide. She died by suicide.

I do not know what your internal struggles were or what you were was facing despite the daily affirmation of "I love you,

Mary," and you would answer back, "Love you too, Mother." Eighteen years afterward, it is still a rollercoaster of emotions. Despite having loving and caring friends, I wanted to dig a hole in my bedroom and never appear again.

Bleeding on the Inside, Smiling on the Outside

Many came as burden bearers, and others as wounded healers, but there were times the truth was never told. As born-again, spirit-filled believers, the truth should always be in us, but countless times from the phone conversations, to greetings we say, "I am okay," though truly sometimes we are bleeding on the inside and smiling on the outside.

A friend, at the lowest moments of trying to navigate the detour, can give lasting remarks and be a game-changer. "It is better a lame dog than a dead one," a friend once said. That does not make sense, but in a way it does because a mother or father in pain may have no reference or a smile. A rude answer reminds a mother of her motherhood. A hard reality required firm faith in God and unwavering hope in Christ.

It is heartbreaking for families regarding the loss of their children and for the parents who have no answers but cling to the only hope, Jesus Christ, with all the answers. Our blessed hope is stated in the book of Titus: "Waiting for our blessed hope, the appearing of the glory of our great God and Savior Jesus Christ, who gave himself for us to redeem us from all lawlessness and to purify for himself a people for his own possession who are zealous for good works" (Titus 2:13–14). Living with eternity in mind gives a better perspective of life! The ambassadorial call and role as a parent is not in vain.

Self-care

Today in our society, there are unwarranted expectations of perfection. Understandably, there can be an increasing amount of stress and anxiety. Many parents are suffering in silence. You as a parent permit yourself to ask for help and allow yourself to say no to something so you can say yes to yourself. It is not selfishness, but you cannot give what you do not have. The need for rest or crying has, in some instances, been viewed as a weakness.

It saddens me to think about what Anita's last moments were like. Anita was a loving single mother of one beautiful daughter, but she gave up. Did she try to reach out to someone? Was there a safe person in her life in whom she could confide? Did she know she could share her struggles with her mom, if not a clergy, mental coach, or therapist?

There is power in asking for help. Many individuals are ready to listen, pray, help, and intervene in any way possible. I have been blessed to have trusted friends who gave a shoulder to cry on. There are angels God has positioned in our parenting crisis seasons when God does not make sense in our literal interpretation.

Don't ask needy people if they need help. "Call me or let me know" is a common phrase, but the best way is to offer help.

The feeling of loneliness in a crowd is no stranger when faced with challenges. There is a good reminder in Hebrews 13:5, "I will never leave you nor forsake you."

Master Deceiver

I discussed earlier that God is the master author of our lives and our children, but Satan is a master deceiver! As parents, we make bad choices, and the guilt trips, medicating to numb pain, and anger outbursts are no excuses.

Delight in Different Talents

Not all will be engineers, directors, lawyers, or singers, but there is a gift and talent for each child. Healthy competitions and hard work are necessary and encouraged, but do not compare children, which can leave a lasting stigma of inadequacy.

"Be the best you can be. Success is the peace of mind that comes as a direct result of knowing that you have done the best you are capable of doing," is my hubby's favorite saying to our children written by retired neurosurgeon Ben Carson. We want to help them work hard, find purpose, delight in their future endeavors, and give their best. Every hurdle your child needs to pass builds them up for the greater one. Repeatedly in Matthew, the parable tells us, "You have been faithful with a few things; I will put you in charge of many things" (Matthew 25:21). It is an encouragement for a right start. As the right person becomes better, then the better person will soon become the best, and he values the reward. But how many times have we failed as parents to recognize our children's talents, and we impose our wishes and the next trending career on our children?

Let the children fulfill God's given purposes and talents. Not all will be follow our footsteps. Nurture their talents.

Parents are so vested in changing the situation and their children. We can't change anyone, and you can't take the responsibility of changing another human being. Still, others can change our flowing in God's love. Be there for them, but don't take responsibility for the outcome. The child may ask, "What do you want? Can I find another job? I accepted the position and wanted the job."

Jesus asked the blind man, "Do you want to get well?" during the healing at the pool. "After this, there was a feast of the Jews, and Jesus went up to Jerusalem. Now there is in Jerusalem near the Sheep Gate a pool, in Aramaic is called Bethesda and which has five covered colonnades. In these lay a multitude of invalids—blind, lame, and paralyzed. One man was there had been an invalid for thirty-eight years. When

Jesus saw him lying there and knew that he had already been there for a long time, he asked him, 'Do you want to be healed?'" (John 5:1–6).

"Do you want to go to church with me?" I had to say yes. We go through a series of decisions regarding what I wanted to do. Children have to make decisions, but do not let the guard down! Know that they are grown, and it is a different ball game! The eaglet has found its wings and can fly. As hard as it is, take care in trying to get vested in their business, bailing them out in the name of help, or taking on the responsibility of them changing. Acknowledge you have limited power.

Righteous Anger

At times, sharing can feel complicated and overbearing due to some stereotypes. "If you cry, you are weak." But I say tears are sometimes healthy and communicate our feelings. The Lord identifies in our parental pain, and this imagery shows God is aware of every tear and identifies with our hurts. The psalmist states, "You have kept count of my tossings; put my tears in your bottle. Are they not in your book?" (Psalm 58:6).

It is okay to be angry so long as it is not sinful, as Apostle Paul states in Ephesians. "Be angry and do not sin; do not let the sun go down on your anger" (Ephesians 4:26). Many times we react to what we see as contrary to our children's behaviors, which is okay. Jesus exhibited righteous anger when he entered the temple and saw the money changers who had made the house of the Lord a den of thieves (John 2:3–16).

There is a need to call out injustices in your child's life, bad choices, detours, and destructions, but be careful not to give opportunity to the devil for uncontrolled anger, venting, and bitterness. You are to build, not tear down, that child. Be gracious and do not grieve; the Holy Spirit of God is with you both.

Vulnerable

"I am sorry" is a magical phrase, but not to most people. With all respect to my late parents, I was blessed and privileged to have loving parents who sacrificed to give us what every parent desires: a solid foundation of Jesus Christ and a good education. With fond memories, I remember the words of my father: "Githomo nokio hingoro" (education is key). It was a fierce parenting that worked and molded me and my siblings into who we are today. I am eternally grateful.

Due to cultural barriers and generational gaps, some instances becomes a challenge to find parents who admit their feelings, faults, and frustrations. I cannot remember sitting around a fireplace and hearing remorseful words from my parents, but I experienced the wrath of their frustrations. Could you and I identify in some parenting instances? With understanding and growth into different dynamics of parenting, certain words and better communication have been a game changer. You and I have vulnerabilities and are wounded and broken people. What's your motivation and expectation? Is it enough to say, "Be careful" or "Just pray"? Not to underscore the power of prayer, but with God-given wisdom, prayer does wonders and miracles. As a biblical counsellor, there are countless sessions of speaking and discussions on a need to shift perspective. We have a need to reevaluate and change our ways of communication. It has been a success, with many people opening up about their deepest hurts to trusted friends—and better still, talking to God deeply without fear.

Apostle Paul, one of the greatest leaders who ever lived and an author of half of the New Testament, is an exemplary leader and example of vulnerability. In his letters to the Corinthians, he states, "We have spoken freely to you, Corinthians; our heart is wide open" (2 Corinthians 6:11). A wide-open heart means being vulnerable in your feelings. Talk, share, and take action.

As parents, authority figures, and leaders in our families, we need to learn to be authentic and vulnerable to our children, giving them a door of opportunity to open up. They should not bottle up feelings, frustrations, and fears, which may get remedies from wrong cures! There are instances of children numbing emotional pain with substances, or they are engaged in wrong relationships as a way of acceptance, which could be curbed earlier by a parent if there was a dialogue.

You and I face the temptations to have more power over people and to be liked more, and our children face the same tricks! With so many competing forces of culture, changing systems, and beliefs, your first line of defense is the Word of God.

From experience, opening your heart to your children, and even in most relationships in life, is effective. You parent from God's power, as Paul expressed in times of hard realities in the following passage: "Indeed, we felt that we had received the sentence of death. But that was to make us rely not on ourselves but on God who raises the dead" (1 Corinthians 1:9). He also admitted failures and faults: "Not that we are sufficient in ourselves to claim anything as coming from us, but our sufficiency is from God" (2 Corinthians 3:5).

In my struggles of communication with my children, the issues were more rooted in my feelings and fears. They were not an easy task but were carefully done. It eases tension, and the children freely express themselves. Apostle Paul admitted his fears and failures when he wrote to the Corinthians: "And I was with you in weakness and in fear and much trembling, and my speech and my message were not in plausible words of wisdom, but in demonstration of the Spirit and of power, so that your faith might not rest in the wisdom of men but in the power of God" (1 Corinthians 2:3–5).

We need more in-depth teachings, explanation, and discussion on these silent topics of stress, suicide, fear, anxiety, screen time, intentional parenting in the study guide, and Bible study of this book. How can you as a parent become more vulnerable and authentic without letting down your guard? Together with Paul, we shall unpack times of parental frustrations. "We are afflicted in every way, but not crushed; perplexed, but not driven to despair" (2 Corinthians 4:8).

Words can speak death or life! Words have power! Words can build up! Words can tear down! What are you declaring over your child? Proverbs 18:21 states, "Death and life are in the power of the tongue has the power of life and those who love it will eats its fruits."

When stakes are high, your words can speak life, or your comments can talk about death in your child's life. Our tongues can build our children, or they can tear them down, and unchecked fires double in size every minute. Do you call them addicts? Lost? Or do you consider them prodigal children who shall return and be found, and you say like Joshua, "But for me and my house, we will serve the Lord" (Joshua 24:15)?

Faith of Grandmother

Paul told Timothy the faith with his grandmother and great-grandmother was still in him. In 2 Timothy 1:5, Paul writes, "I am reminded of your sincere faith, a faith that dwelt first in your grandmother Lois and your mother Eunice and, now, I am sure, dwells in you as well." These women were responsible for passing their faith on to the next generation. A grand heritage was passed on from my praying grandmother, who as I stated earlier, entered eternal rest at 106 years in September 2020. That is a great reminder that the Lord is with your life and the same characteristics of heroes of faith are worth emulating. The seeds you sow today are not in vain! The baton of faith will be passed when you are home. As Paul wrote to the Corinthians, "Yes, we are of good courage, and we would rather be away from the body and at home with the Lord" (2 Corinthians 5:8). That is a great reminder to live with eternity in mind. Yes, we are not home yet!

Parents: Teachers of Culture

Jesus's teachings and prayers explain a believer's culture is second to none. "I have given them your word, and the world has hated them, because they are not of the world just as I am of the world. I do not ask that you take them out of the world but keep them from the evil ones. They are not of the world, just as I am of the world" (John 17:14–16).

Satan rules the system of the world. We don't want to be a part of that, right? Awesomely enough, Jesus says that those who believe in him are no longer a part of that cosmos. Sin has no power over us, and we don't have to be trapped by the evil principles of the world. Even more astonishing is that belief in Christ causes us to change. Our hearts will be less interested in the things of the world as we strive to be more like Jesus.

Therefore if we aren't ruled by Satan and sin, that's great, but we still live here! Yeah, not so great. But Jesus has given us freedom from that evil, remember? We may be physically present ("in the world"), but we don't have to be a part of its values ("of the world"; John 17:14–16). We're set apart from the wickedness of the cosmos as we seek to live holy, righteous lives.

Better Than Your Parents

To say I want to be better than my parents may sound conceited and ungrateful, but from a different perspective with the changing culture. I would need to write a book of my loving parents and sacrificial parenting to see me and my siblings get wings like the eagles. Is it a different season for our children? Definitely. There is need for healing and teachable moments so I do not carry emotional baggage into my parenting journey.

Changing Culture

Not long ago, a mother hired a stripper to perform at his thirteen-year-old daughter's birthday party. Unfortunately, this type of behavior is no longer as shocking as it might once have been. Our culture continues to worsen because of sin. Many children are being exposed to warped sexual images every day, over and over. Worse still, during these challenging times of COVID-19, the only communication avenue is online.

We cannot afford to sit back and allow the dark side of culture to become a significant influence in our children's lives. When I speak to my teenage daughter, I often say, "I wouldn't want to be your age. You experience a more negative cultural influence than I did."

When I was growing up, I was free to walk to and from school before going to boarding school back in Kenya. I was free to play with my neighbors and visit the neighborhood and village. All the neighbors and villagers knew each other and watched out for each other. A neighbor would even punish a child before reporting it to the parents; we had village accountability.

Back then, teens were still teens and children were still children, because they still experimented with behaviors that weren't good or healthy for them.

After all, for those who were not believers in Christian unions (CU), even in those days, sex, drugs, rock and roll, and discos were part of teen culture. But compared to what teenagers face today, it seemed like a much more peaceful world back then.

I am a very optimistic person, and my faith in the Lord keeps me in check, but our children are growing up in a mess. We can blame it on the media, globalization, and a host of other issues, but today's culture has robbed teenagers of their innocence.

We can discuss it, complain, protest, and fight the status quo, but in the end, as parents we are the ones who must make the adjustments and fight to keep a biblical worldview in front of our children. By the end of the week or month, before you know it, cultural issues and trends will have emerged, such as TikTok, Snapchat, and others. Not all cultural changes are bad. When migrating to America twenty years ago from Kenya, we faced culture shock, which I still deal with today. Many cultures are simply different.

Children and specifically teens crave relationships and community, but they find them in different ways through different mediums than previous generations. It's not their fault that society is rapidly changing, and they have to find their way in the world because it is not as we hope it could be.

Every year some college globally publishes a mindset list. This collection list of cultural reference points shows how the generations have fewer and fewer shared experiences with each new college freshman class. For today's college students, it's a different ball game than our times.

Google doc has always been around.

They have not seen a paper airplane ticket.

They have not seen a real magician.

TikTok is their entertainment.

Billy Graham, Wangari Maathai, Kofi Anan, Mother Teresa, and Dr. Martin King Jr. have always been dead.

My husband showed me a cartoon that showed a teenager lying on the floor of his bedroom. He was holding a smartphone, FaceTiming, and listening to Pandora music on his computer with the television in the background. There were video games and many more gadgets around the room. As he FaceTimed with his friend, he answered a question about how he was feeling: "Soo bored." He sighed. "What about you?"

The response from his friend: "Same."

We got bored when we were eleven, fifteen, and eighteen, but we never face the enormous onslaught of an ever-changing culture.

Parents, stay informed on trends and culture. That is crucial for having meaningful conversations with your kids on identity, anxiety, depression, and addiction. Become a student of the culture. Raising a child nowadays is demanding and an extraordinarily complex duty, requiring flexibility, judgment, and delicate balancing.

Dr. Jim Burns, in his book *Understanding Your Teen,* says you should get your arms around shifting minds. One of the better ways to help your child navigate the issues of adolescence is to become a student of the culture. The goal is not to become an anti-culture critic because we parents of different descent have challenges and fondly refer to things "during my days back home." Does that sound familiar? All is said in finality, but it can deeply wound children with unanswered questions.

If you carefully look back and reflect on the changing world trend and the parental roles you have to deal with, you will know you must stay informed on the trends and the changing culture.

Many parents are still working on this, but you can get your arms around who influences our children in today's culture and dialogue. Simply listen! As a parent who wants to be a student of the culture and keep your arms around the shifting mindsets, you will want to look at issues, particularly during these challenging times of COVID-19, when we are faced with countless roles: the principle, the teacher, the minister, the teacher, the breadwinner, and more. Multiplied grace to you, and keep up the excellent job. The seeds you plant now will soon bear much fruit.

New studies show a link between teen drug and alcohol use and increased sexual activity. This includes teen social media, faith beliefs, an increase in teenage girls' suicide rates. Mental health issues are on the rise. Alcohol dependence is linked to the age of one's first drink. Mothers have their most challenging times when children are in middle school. Our teenage girls are unhappy with their bodies.

No doubt, this world needs children who can stand out for Christ rather than fit in. They are not vulnerable, naive, gullible, and isolated as they grow. As believers, don't we all need to stand out for Jesus and not conform to the patterns and systems of the world? Let those reflective years you spend with your children be filled with joy, knowing you did your best with the God-given tools as you partnered with him to mold and nurture them. They will soon grow and go.

Sin creates the gap, but Jesus bridges it!

Keeping up with Cultural Issues

Parents, this digital generation is different from what it was growing up for you and me. It is important to get our arms around *who* influences this generation. Your children have unspoken issues hitting the headlines daily, with identity posing a significant challenge. There are issues with mental health, depression, eating disorders, suicide, alcoholism, and drug addiction. The message is painted on the wall. Have a dialogue to seek practical solutions and save a generation. Parents, you must keep up with the latest cultural trends and how they are affecting your children.

Today and through history, we witness humanity, every culture, seeking solutions to life's challenges and difficulties. Generations offering their models and self-made philosophies with no personal or interpersonal tangible solutions, but there is a downward, escalating spiral plaguing our society, especially our children. The body of Christ and homes of believers are sailing in the same boat. There are increasing cases of fear, worry, depression, substance abuse, and broken families, with many other cases leading to suicide, distress, and cases of hopelessness.

Mental Health Determinants

The Bible says we perish because of lack of knowledge (Hosea 4:6).

According to the World Health Organization, about 10–20 percent of adolescents globally experience mental health conditions, with no diagnosis or treatment, or it is undertreated. The risk factors for stress levels is due to a need for greater autonomy, peer pressure, and increase in the use of social media, distorting their identity perception and setting unrealistic expectations for their future. The hard reality is that harsh parenting and violence has exacerbated the mental health cases in children.

Biblical Mental Health Solutions

Parents, there is need for unlocking meaningful conversations with your children and reflecting on your approach. Maybe there is a need for a second chance change, a prodigal son experience with God the Father. Repent and be the loving, encouraging, kind parent your child deserves.

In my parental journey, biblical counseling, and health promotion as a believer in the Lord Jesus Christ, I can attest the one and only source that identifies the causes and gives solutions to these problems, behaviors, communication, attitudes, and hardened hearts is the Bible. It was written over seventeen centuries and endured over two thousand years, and it offers the basis for a vital and abundant life.

Gen Z Spiritual Investment

A youth pastor ministering at a discipleship youth weekend from my church gave staggering, eye-opening, and heartbreaking statistics regarding our youth and impressed upon us the urgency to reach a generation in danger. Parents, we have a role and a part to play. Generation Z is more atheist or agnostic, and only 4 percent have a biblical worldview, with 10 percent identifying with Christ! One out of three are agonistic with no reference to God. Suicide rates have increased for ages ten to fourteen. These are depressing statistics. The downward spiral may lead to what is written the book of Judges: "And all that generation also were gathered to their fathers. And there arose another generation after them who did not know the LORD or the work that he had done for Israel" (Judges 2:10).

Hope For Gen Z

There is hope, and we shall not be weary over our children. You have to introduce them to Jesus. I love what the psalmist says in Psalm 145:4, "One generation shall commend your works to another, and shall declare your mighty acts." We have to spoon-feed them and must not stop being territorial in saying, "This is my ministry." Let our children be our imitators as we follow Christ. As Paul said in 1 Corinthians 1:11, "Be imitators of me, as I am of Christ." Tell them, "Come work with me." Your child does not just show up but wants to be part of a bigger thing!

We parents have to "stir them up." Is your child walking in a loving home, or are you rebuking their dressing, behavior, and relationships?

There is help and a need for revival. We can reach a generation in danger, a generation in need of a Savior. Set a fire for Jesus. There is a real spiritual warfare in the lives of our children. Their emotions are affected, and their souls and minds are impacted. Our children need Jesus to be their Savior, King, and Master over their lives.

How do we stir our children? Find ways to encourage them in times of crisis. I am currently writing this book in a crisis within a crisis! There is a global pandemic with so many cases of mental health issues.

We have to go to God on their behalf and intercede. The one we pray to is able. He is a God who cares and listens. We have to trust God as we do our part. "Blessed is the man who trusts in the LORD, whose trust is the LORD" (Jeremiah 17:7).

May the Lord help you spiritually invest in the lives of your children. Engage them in Bible studies, youth camps, Vocational

Bible School(VBS), retreats, and discipleship events, Let them serve and learn servanthood leadership. Do not say they are young. Remember Paul's message to Timothy: "Let no one despise you for your youth, but set the believers an example in speech, in conduct, in love, in faith, in purity" (1 Timothy 4:12).

Intentionally observant

A major part of being a student of culture is to watch what teens and children are watching. Discuss it with them, and either watch it with them or later. Get critical insights into their culture, which will give you a new perspective on issues they are thinking or talking about. Be intentionally observant when you attend an event or see their interactions with peers on Zoom, FaceTime, and chats. Be the parent who volunteers at youth activities, chaperones, or drives. In a nutshell, we can learn so much about our children when we are in their territory.

Communication

"Mom, you are not listening to me!" That is respectfully stated but is a work in progress for many of us parents. Listening is the best way to understand your children and their cultural influences. With a teenage daughter and young adults, I have learned over the years that they don't want Mom and Dad to act like teenagers and participate in their activities. However, it is okay to ask what is happening in their world as long as the questions are not judgmental.

I have learned to find time to casually ask my teen and young adults about topics such as school, sex, drugs, and alcohol use on the school campus. During this COVID-19 season, homeschooling has presented an excellent opportunity to interact better, not to mention work on communication skills.

Spiritual Wealth

My late paternal grandmother was the epitome of living by the book—the Bible, or *Kirikaniro* as she fondly called it in our mother tongue. "Amazing Grace" (Utugi wa Magegania) was her favorite hymn.

What was her secret for a long life and parenting with sanity for several children and over one hundred grandchildren and great-grandchildren? Did every child and grandchild follow her footsteps? In a perfect world, that is ideal, but we don't live there now! But the seeds were sown, and if anyone deviated from the truth, they knew there was something wrong. Today, the words of wisdom from my praying grandma live with her family and the thousands of lives she impacted. Philippians 4:4 is a favorite verse and family legacy: "Rejoice in the Lord always; again I will say, rejoice. Let your reasonableness be known to everyone. The Lord is at hand."

Similarly my late maternal grandmother cucu Rahab home with the Lord started a great work in my family through prayers, sang hymns early in the morning when sweeping her compound .Today these memories resonates with many of her grandchildren many ministers of the gospel. She was fearless, praying grandma, mentioned all her children by name and lifted them before the Lord! A rich Spiritual legacy.

Counterculture

In *Counter Culture, New York Times* bestselling author David Platt shows Christians how to actively take a stand on such issues as poverty, sex trafficking, marriage, abortion, racism, and religious liberty—and challenges us to become passionate, unwavering voices for Christ.

Today, parents can't give up and can't back down. They must invest spiritually in their children. Parents can make a difference they are proactive. Here are some tips.

Set Parental Standards.

When it comes to culture, help children set standards and develop a sound biblical grid to measure morals and values. Everything should not be a fight. It pays off later, and when children become responsible adults, they appreciate parents' expectations and the consequences of choices. It takes intentionality for parents to promote restraints and to teach children a biblical worldview.

When it comes to the unknown, I will fill my spiritual well with the truth of God's Word, taking caution of the many theories and information on social media. These are teachable moments with family devotion and study time, refocus time, and bonding time.

The Bible says in 2 Timothy 2:15, "Do your best to present yourself to God as one approved, a worker who does not need to be ashamed, rightly handling the word of truth."

Counterculturally

God says it's vital, though culture says otherwise. Will children always agree with parents? No, though they will know your boundaries and standards even if they rebel. The majority of children want to please their parents despite not acting like it.

Encourage Positive Peer Influence

Peer pressure doesn't always have to be negative. Positive peer influence is a mighty influence. The Bible says, "Bad company corrupts good character" (1 Corinthians 15:33), but the opposite is also true: good company encourages good feeling. Healthy friendships will help your children deal with unhealthy cultural influences. Do everything you can to know your children's friends and help foster positive activities. Zoom collective teen devotions with parental guidance, cooking and baking classes, or simply to chill and giggle.

A positive school environment tends to have much more

strength in overcoming negative cultural temptations. A good idea is to foster participation in church youth groups. They can provide a fun, spiritually strong environment with healthy role models and opportunities for quality friendships. Never underestimate the power of positive peer influence.

Foster Spiritual Growth

Research shows that adolescence is a season when teens have questions about their faith and drift from church. But are you guilty as charged, like me, for replacing dialogue and listening with yelling at a deaf ear?

My fellow parents, our children are in search of answers too. They have emotional wounds. They need healing from pain. They desire to build good relationships. How do you stay engaged with your struggling teenager or young adult when you yell? Teens who develop their spiritual disciplines and stay involved in church are much less at risk. However, even with the best applications, some children turn out the complete opposite.

Remember that as a parent, you cannot live a spiritual life for your children. Nagging them into a deeper relationship with God has never worked. However, you can build a home environment that fosters spiritual growth and gives your children plenty of opportunities to mature and apply their faith to the culture.

Tough Love

Children can be extremely committed to developing and maturing their spiritual lives despite the cultural pressures they face. However, keep in mind that their faith may look different than yours. To my fellow Christian parents from Diaspora, a word of encouragement: Due to cultural shock, the style and disciplines we apply may have gone sour. Our African American children may not understand our worship ways and feel forced to attend church as a ritual rather than as an assembly of fellowship. However, the God of yesterday, today, and tomorrow remains the firm foundation of our homes. The book of Hebrews states, "Not neglecting to meet together, as is the habit of some is; but encouraging one another: and all the more, as you see the day drawing near" (Hebrews 10:25).

Embracing Teachable Moments

One of my son's favorite thing to say to his small sister is, "Find Jesus for yourself. Mom, let her know the why. Why do we go to church? Why the suffering? Why the no? Why the anointing oil at the door? Why? It is an endless list."

Surprisingly, I swallowed my pride and embraced my teachable moments. Children seek answers too!

Parents, you area the first responders to your child; otherwise the wicked world will teach them harshly. They will answer their awesome why the wrong way—with lifelong consequences.

5

Grace Abounds

You were created to be dependent. God welcomes your dependency with his Grace, so why would you want to go it on your own?
—Paul Tripp

I'm sometimes the queen of difficulty, in the sense that I can run most of my life without much help. I want my independence, and when things fall through the cracks and the outcome is off from what I expected, frustration kicks in. Then I am not the best wife, mother, friend, or colleague. It is not intentional to be difficult, but the autonomy and self-sufficiency struggle with my new creation from a very young age.

You and I are in a long journey of parenting. We are carriers of God's precious creatures and gifts, but we have no control over the outside of God's authority. We are partners.

In the same way, our children grow into this autonomy stage and believe that they can live their lives as they please. They dictate when to wake up or go to sleep, when to eat, and when to go to bed. They can have temper tantrums! What about teenagers who think they have an opinion and answer to everything? How about the ones cruising the highways at night who feel entitled to knock at your door in the wee hours of the morning?

Parents, raising great children and enjoying the process comes with its challenges! I suspect there are times you and I have missed out on our calling and dependence on the power of the gospel and God's unfailing grace. In some instances, the gospel is not always the foundation and response to the child whose bedroom looks like a hurricane has hit it.

Honestly, you and I have a past. You cannot change the past, but you can choose to not live in that misery! The detours and the pain are loud. My scars and your brokenness tell a story that says we are overcomers. There is no condemnation to those in Christ Jesus! How can you count it pure joy amid parenting turmoil? This is a point I made in the previous chapter on the storms of life-detours.

To say God has placed extreme value on you as a parent is an understatement. As Paul stated in 2 Corinthians 12:9, "My Grace is sufficient for my power is made perfect in weakness. Therefore I will boast all more gladly of my weaknesses, so that the power of my Christ may rest upon me."His Grace abounds.

A Tale of Two Cities

Our children might fulfill our dreams through us. Do you believe it? I made that statement as my son narrated his Israel tour. As I read and better understood, Israel has two central water bodies, the Sea of Galilee in the north and the Dead Sea to the south. My son's picture of him floating on the Dead Sea made me more interested in its tourist attraction operation. About two million gallons of water flow into the Dead Sea daily, but none goes out. It contains approximately thirty grams of salt per liter. Is that not amazing? For that reason, there are no reported cases of drowning. Consequently, there is so much salt and so many minerals that one floats. Only a tumbleweed is in existence, and there is a barren shore that exudes death.

In contrast, the Sea of Galilee is brimming with life, fishing, and vegetation.

The Spiritual Reality of Humanity

As my son calmly told us about his exciting journey and experience of Israel, I did my best to be a good listener, work in progress, and listen. Proverbs 18:13 states, "The One who answers before he listens—this is foolishness and disgrace for him." Lord, have mercy! A small diversion, but necessary!

From my son's narrative of Israel, I could not stop thinking of the analogy of humanity's spiritual reality being just like the Sea of Galilee, which continually breathes life and fruitfulness, and the Dead Sea, which lives death and uselessness. In the same way, there are two types of people: the person in the original Adam, and the person in the second Adam, Jesus Christ.

How does this analogy apply to parenting? Our children need the gospel—not more than you and I need it, but differently. Don't we all sin and fall short? Grace is an undeserved gift. You and I have been shown grace, and we can display it as a beautiful trait to our children. It is freely given. Therefore, say the blessing!

It's not the checkbook, the yelling, the relocation, or the number of phone calls we make in search of answers. In thriving for grace based-parenting, God calls children a gift and a blessing. The psalmist states, "Children are a gift from the Lord; they are a reward from him. Children born to a young man are like arrows in a warrior's hands" (Psalm 127:3–5).

The best example of God's grace is shown through Jesus Christ. The following are hard but necessary verses on sin.

> For, sin indeed was in the world through before the law was given, but sin is not counted but sin is not counted where there is no law. Yet death

> reigned from Adam's to Moses, even over those whose sinning was not like the transgression of Adam, who was the type of the One who was to come. But the free gift is not like the trespass. For if the many died through one man trespass, much more have grace of God and the free gift by the grace of the one man, Jesus Christ, abounded for many! (Romans 5:13–15)

Adam was the first man created, along with his wife, Eve, on the sixth day. They became ancestors of humanity, but Adam's choice to disobey God brought sin and death into the world and strained his relationship between him and God. He failed to keep God's command: "But of the tree of the knowledge of good and evil, you shall not eat, for the day that you eat of it you shall surely die" (Genesis 2:17). Apostle Paul gives a fair comparison and contrast on Adam's work with Jesus Christ, giving a clear understanding that what Jesus did was far greater than what Adam did and therefore was justified by faith.

Our culture of raising children competes with us, with no preparation for this high calling. I grew up in a loving home and was privileged in various ways, but to say I did not taste the cane and some hurtful words would be a lie! My well-meaning father, an authoritarian with a military background, required obedience to strict and tight standards of behavior. The controlled environment helped shape my six siblings and me, who were well nurtured but not with some consequences. My loving mother did not mince her words, but thank God they were mostly well seasoned!

To say God has placed extreme value on you as a parent is an understatement. In healthcare, there is a common phrase: "Assumption is a killer." A nurse cannot assume a patient received specific care or medication, and that is why there is transfer or handing over through a shift report, for the continuum of care.

Are you solely blaming your past mistakes on your parents?

No, but as parents, assuming your children have a built-in moral structure is deceiving. As seen in the story of first Adam, children are born with a corrupted nature, requiring protection more than control. Your child needs grace more than management!

Wake-up Call

For two years during my biblical counselor's training, I was in search of a more profound theological and practical way of living, specifically parenting a wayward child and loving the unlovable like me. As I sat in every class and drove home every Tuesday night from the college, the words brought great conviction, and a part of me wanted to sit, scream, sob, cry, and confess my shortcomings and failures as a parent. The other part of me wanted me to call with excitement for the great insights and principles learned regarding the big picture of life through the gospel's lens—and better still, a better parenting worldview.

At this point in my parenting journey, I may be painting a picture of a perfect parent with the "how to parent" strategies. My fellow parent, that's not true. We are imperfect parents, with a perfect God calling you and me to fulfill his will in our parenting journey. I have learned through my three decades of parenting, and vendetta leads only to frustration. When my parental outcomes are not met, nothing makes sense. Even when knowing or quoting scriptures, parenting calls for the obedience of God's Word through grace and a wake-up call to humanity's spiritual reality.

Fear or Concern?

Were my children daily recipients of the grace that I enjoy daily from a loving God? Was I peaceful and graceful when my children were the hardest to love? Adapting a fear-based parenting model or high-control parenting became more detrimental and did not display Christlike character. The epistle of John states in 1 John 4:18–19, "There is no fear in love. But perfect love casts out fear for fear has to do with punishment. and whoever fears has not made perfected in love. We love because he first loved us." Like any other well-meaning parent, I fell short in some areas, not all. Remember, it is a journey!

God's Design for Parenting

Parenting was a desire right from a young age, after seeing my mother bring us up, nurture us, and provide for us around the fireplace. Is anyone prepared or taught to parent? Growing up came with certain expectations and goals; going to school and high achievement was not an option. Going to church every Sunday and preparing to recite back scriptures to my father was not an option either, and there were many more parental expectations for us. That unconsciously built in me parental confusion for an ultimate authority and ownership of children to parents. I somehow lost sight of parenting's role and became more reactive than goal-oriented. I submitted to God's supreme Lordship, trusting him fully in my parenting journey and not fretting.

A wayward child's experience did not come without a mind shift of a surrender mentality that led more to God's design. I learned to appreciate the small chaotic moments, the almost insignificant moments, giving parenting a location and address. The significance was not just in the school grades, achievements, superb activities, and juggling from one sport to another. More meaning was found in the unplanned car drive moments, the cooking laughter moments.

Parents, as you daily meet your children's needs, know that God has given you a privileged position of influence over their lives to guide their hearts. From their young age to adulthood, you can help them experience his love and blessings, and you can be a parent after God's own heart, spreading the fragrance of Christ in your home. Soak yourself in the sustaining grace of God. Saturate your mind with God's Word. It gives comfort, strengthens, is soothing to your soul, and energizes you to stay on the journey.

A healthy home builds a healthy society and nation!

Parental Call with a Command

I did all that was humanly possible, what was well-meaning, and what seemed right in my own eyes to lay out expectations for and from my children, but I was the author of their lives. Their care was entrusted to me. Like any other parent, I was not unique in my deliberate expectations of meeting both physical and inner needs in the anticipation that they would grow up to be visionaries, trust in a better future, long for a greater good, and ultimately put their trust in God.

I had a realization that children are God's possession, and he created them for a purpose. As a parent, you are to faithfully submit to his authority, nurture children, and care for them in God's way, not yours.

Did God Stay Silent?

Is it possible for God to be silent to our parental storms? For emphasis, as discussed elsewhere, with all the well-meaning parental intentions, there are times you have the Bible verses, Bible slices, and Bible sermons, but in your mind you are saying, "Lord, I believe, but help my unbelief." There are times you say, "Lord, in your Word you there is no temptation that I cannot overcome, but with several years passing, the suffering and anguish is more than one can bear. I am disappointed! Lord, are you still there?"

The emotional pain can brew for some years, but taking on a different parental perspective changes one's way of thinking. Branding oneself as the final authority over a child's life is forgetting we as parents are ambassadors called with a job description and resources from the Creator of our children.

Parent as an Ambassador

From Merriam-Webster's Dictionary, an ambassador is a diplomatic official of the highest rank, sent by one sovereign, government, or state to another as its resident representative to represent it on a mission, such as for negotiating a treaty. A parent's journey and confessions are directed and shaped by personal interests, needs, and cultural perspectives. Little did it occur to me that my ambassador parental role was to carry out my Father's will to raise the children entrusted in my care. As parents, your primary task is to be an ambassador of the kingdom of God. Despite the children's outcome, your desire should always be to please the Lord. Apostle Paul states, "Therefore, we are ambassadors for Christ, God making his appeal through us. We implore you on behalf of Christ, be reconciled to God" (2 Corinthians 5:20).

Protecting or Preparing Your Child: Teaching Responsibility without Guilt

The struggle was protecting children in their helplessness and preparing them to be independent in the ambassadorial parental role. From conception to about eighteen years, they are in an age of protection and preparation so they can thrive and flourish for God in a dark world.

Your Child's Responsibility and Freedom to Make Mistakes

To say a children have to bear the consequences of their choices may sound harsh, but every choice has consequences. God gives us freedom to obey or disobey. To stay in God's will, the scriptures states, "And if it is evil in your eyes to serve the LORD, choose this day whom you will serve, whether the gods your fathers served in the region beyond the River, or the gods of the Amorites in whose land you dwell. But as for me and my house, we will serve the LORD" (Joshua 24:15).

To reverse the consequences, one has to be anchored and established to the source of life and not be bound by sin. Believe in Christ and allow Him to be Lord and Savior, made new in living the life of Jesus by the power of the Holy Spirit, as written by Paul in his letter to the Romans. "For "everyone who calls on the name of the Lord will be saved" (Romans 10:13). Revelation 3:20 states, "Behold, I stand at the door and knock. If anyone hears my voice and opens the door, I will come in to him and eat with him, and he with me."

The parental role is ideal needed for children to process the best and meet their needs, including security, strength, and significance, love, purpose, and hope. But the lack of giving children freedom to be different and make mistakes is not helpful. There is a realization that a legalistic, fear-based family undermines a child's ability to develop a commitment to the righteousness that comes from a deep love for God.

Awkward Periods of Parenting

I want to clarify that what I am writing now is a work in process, with some struggles but with a different mind shift! The first twenty years of parenting were faced with a sense of ownership. I was a poor ambassador of God's grace driven by anxiety and fear, not faith!

I wanted microwave results rather than a long-term

transformation through my children's molding and transformative years. First Peter 5:7 states, "Cast all your anxiety on him because he cares for you." God did not make sense in my anxious moments, but he did and still does when I take my ambassadorial role to submit to God's rescue and power.

No Condemnation

Jesus Christ is the same yesterday, today, and forever. That is not a cliché! There are often different voices from your mind, and many more reminding you of your past and failures due to parental outcomes. Let me be candid and say some voices and actions are not worth entertaining. They call for discernment. For example, there are times the devil reminds you of your past. Remind him of his future in hell and tell him that it is written in the gospel of John, "So if the Son sets you free, you will be free indeed" (John 8:36). "Therefore, if anyone is in Christ, he is a new creation. The old has passed away; behold, the new has come" (2 Corinthians 5:17). Apostle Paul says, "Three times I pleaded with the Lord about this, that it should leave me. But he said to me, 'My grace is sufficient for you, for my power is made perfect in weakness.' Therefore I will boast all the more gladly of my weaknesses, so that the power of Christ may rest upon me" (2 Corinthians 12:8–9).

If you are in the detours, don't give up. Simply look up!

For many years, I would have argued the Christian walk, God's Word, and prayer were different entities. However I have realized they are essentials, like food, water, and clothing. They are necessary, they are vital, and they propel us as parents.

Sin Consequences

> Sin will take you farther than you want to go,
> keep you longer than you want to stay, and cost
> you more than you want to pay.
>
> —Ravi Zacharias

Sadly, all humankind bears the consequences of Adam's sin. Who likes the doctrine of representation? Do you want to be represented by Adam? It is not fair! The model by Adam is none of my desire!

After working as a hospice crisis care nurse, nothing could be nearer than the truth on sin and the dire consequences of physical death. Apostle Paul said to the Romans, "For if, because of one man's trespass, death reigned through that one man, much more will those who receive the abundance of grace and the gift of righteousness reign in life through the one man Jesus Christ" (Romans 5:17). That is a sobering reality, that death still reigns. Remember the next time you set your eyes on a hearse or a mortuary, death still reigns! However, understanding our origin of sin changes our entire position. We used to be in Adam, but now we are in Christ. Grace reigns over all!

Common Christian teaching is that grace is unmerited favor. Our loving Father's empowering class gave to humanity by sending his Son, Jesus Christ, to die on a cross, therefore securing our eternal salvation from sin. Within Christianity, there are different concepts of how grace is attained. His grace doesn't just free us from the punishment of sin; it also frees us from the presence and power of sin. God's grace accepts us even though we've sinned, and it empowers us to overcome evil.!

Just as in anything good, the opposite is wrong. Without grace, it's damaging, and for the unredeemed, it is damning. Paul, in his letter to the Romans, stated, "For the wages of sin is death, but the free gift of God is eternal life in Christ Jesus our Lord" (Romans 6:23).

Can we continue in sin and yet grace may abound? Paul replies with a resounding, "God forbid!" Specifically he says, "By no means! How can we die to sin still live in it?" (Romans 6:2). To desire to continue in sin shows a misunderstanding of this abundant grace and love—and a contempt for Jesus's sacrifice.

Is it not the same God who saved and delivered you so that you can do the same for your child? He shows no favoritism. Romans 2:11–12 states, "For God shows no partiality, For all who have sinned without the law will also perish without the law, and all who have sinned under the law will be judged by the law."

Dr. James Dobson, a host of one of my favorite morning radio shows, *Family Talk with Family*, once taught an unforgettable session and urged listeners to memorize the following:

> Sin will take you farther than you wanna go,
> Sin will keep you longer than you want to stay,
> Sin will cost you more than want to pay!

Addictions and Consequences

Addictions strip minds and ruin relationships. There is a spiritual nature in addiction. The biblical term the world uses for addiction is *stronghold*, referring to the spiritual nature of addiction. So how do you sanely and gracefully deal with a child's addiction? Vintage Vivids could not have neen further fro the truth in his statement "when you finally learn that a perrson's behavior has more to do with their internal struggle than it ever did with you,you will learn Grace"Grace to to love with the father's steadfast love !Is it as easy as A,B,C?Let's dive in deeper not God's undiluted word.

Gift By Grace

Sin has caused the high negative impacts, the bad choices of friends, the bad temper, the substance abuse, different sexual orientation, elopement, and disruption of communication. These take the child further than a wrecked life. The cost is hefty, characterized by conflict, violence, emotional chaos, and fear, leading to a dysfunctional family.

As a parent, it should not be a surprise that your child has consequences of Adam's sin before birth. Worse still, there is a level of selfishness! As explained by Paul clearly in an earlier passage, all humans are in Adam. He further explains the result or consequence of Adam's sin. As our representative, Adam sinned, and his sin was applied to every person who has ever lived or will ever live.

Paul summarizes and explains this thought in Romans 5:12, "Therefore, just as through one man sin entered into the world, and death through sin, and so death spread to all men because all sinned."

Just as sin entered the world through one man, and death through sin, in this way death came to all men because all sinned. Even so, through one act of righteousness, there resulted in the justification of life to all men. Paul writes that sin entered the world through one man and spread to all men. But here there is hope, as explained in Romans 5:15, "But the gift is not like the trespass. For if many died through one man's trespass, much more have the Grace of God and the gift by the grace of that one man Jesus Christ abounded for many."

Wage of Sin

Understanding the consequences of Adam's sin came to bear on all humankind, and it explains our children do not go into the world with the innocence of seeking God and righteousness. They have the worldly desire of sinful nature from you, as a parent. You got it from your parent—it is not learned but inbred!

Is sin only to specific children? No, it is universal. "Through sin, death spread to all men. For just as through the disobedience of the one man the many were made sinners, so also through the obedience of the one man the many will be made righteous" (Roman's 5:19).

That means children will pursue sin if not addressed. However, truth should be communicated sincerely with a grace-based atmosphere, encouraging children to constructively talk about troubling issues they are working on, without worrying about the cost through open communication. This leads to an enjoyable childhood, teenage years, and adulthood with few regrets.

This is a practical truth you may struggle with, but with the power of the Holy Spirit within you, it is possible to have the freedom to be candid. Sin is a thief, destroyer, and punisher. It is Satan's way of keeping the believers of Jesus Christ from walking in God's will and enjoying God's best for our lives. For the unbeliever, sin is Satan's way of keeping that person forever separated from God. They are spending eternity with the devil because they never accepted Jesus as their Lord and Savior. We well understand that sin was brought into the world when Adam and Eve ate the forbidden fruit and lied to God afterward.

In his infinite mercy and unconditional love, God sent his only begotten Son, Jesus to carry and suffer the cost of our sins as a repayment of a corrupt, lost, dying society so we could have eternal life and forgiveness through the Son to the Father.

Jesus's sacrifice and loving gift to us did not wipe out sin in the world. Satan and his army still are determined to destroy, rob, divide, kill, and more important keep people from accepting Jesus Christ as their Lord and Savior. The Apostle Paul said, "For the wages of sin is death" (Romans 6:23). Paul said this thousands of years ago, but it still holds today. If left unchecked and not dealt with, sin destroys families, marriages, and friendships, and it ultimately leaves us down a road of pure heartbreak and misery. More important, if people have has not accepted Christ as their Lord and Savior, it means they are forever separated from God and Jesus, which means the fiery lake of hell awaits the unbelievers.

Our children will sin in our lives because we are born in the flesh and are natural-born sinners. The saving grace for believers is that Jesus paid the hefty price of our sins on the cross. On the cross, Jesus's death paid the same heavy price for nonbelievers because it gave them a chance to ask for forgiveness and ask Jesus to come into their hearts so they can be born again into Christ, with their sins wiped clean.

We as parents do not let unresolved sin and the continuous sin of our children keep us from a relationship with Jesus Christ. We must not allow evil to destroy our families, marriages, relationships with others, and ourselves, because sin takes us down a road a cold, lonely, dark road of devastation, destruction, and possibly death. The commandments are clear: "Thou shall not ..." Even though we are not perfect, we still should try to honor and obey God's law for us. God knows sin is a thief and enforcer of misery, and if left unchecked, it will keep us from enjoying God's best for us. If sin is a constant struggle for you, ask God to forgive you and help you overcome the sin that has a stranglehold on your life. Please do not let sin destroy you or your dreams, goals, and families. More important, do not let sin rob you of the opportunity to know the Son and Father as Savior. There is power in the blood of Christ for forgiveness, and we can defeat and overcome sin in our lives. It starts with accepting Jesus as our Lord and Savior. Then it is confession and admission of our sins. After that, it is trusting, obeying God through his Word and the Holy Spirit that resides in our hearts to defeat evil. Trust God fully and leave the consequences for him to handle it. Remember, you cannot do it alone!

Sinful Heart

I have often gone off track by focusing my efforts on controlling my children's behavior, correcting the external behavior with some treats of discipline in case of misbehavior. We said discipline should be accorded when necessary. That is all well and good, but little did I realize the heart condition of children exhibits in their behavior. I am not a stranger to signs and symptoms of an underlying diagnosis in healthcare. Therefore a sinful heart breeds immoral behavior!

Is This Curable?

It is not enough or appropriate to isolate children from harmful influences. Do not get me wrong: as parents, we must protect and nurture. Teaching children to be wise and discerning when confronted with temptation and evil is more productive at a certain age into adulthood. Otherwise, we may be training hypocrites to act appropriately when parents are nearby.

Your Child's Heart

There needs to be a balance so children do not feed unselfish behavior in the name of self-esteem. Children should love themselves; they should not be self-centered and deny themselves. It is unbiblical. "Then he said to them all: 'Whoever wants to be my disciple must deny themselves and take up their cross daily and follow Me" (Luke 9:23). Looking around this world, the only remedy for our children's sinful nature is new birth. Jesus was clear on this when he told Nicodemus, "That which is born of the flesh is flesh, and that which is born of the Spirit is spirit ... Therefore, you must be born again" (John 3:6–7). "Born of the flesh," children born with sin have no power over the bondage of sin by themselves! They need a helper, the Holy Spirit, to work in the truth and light of the gospel! As stated by Paul to the Romans, "For those who live according to the flesh set their minds on the things of the flesh, but those who live according to the Spirit set their minds on the things of the spirit. For to set the mind on the flesh is death, but to set to mind on the Spirit is life and peace. For the mind that is set on the flesh is hostile to God, for it does not submit to God's law: indeed, it cannot. Those who are in the realm of the flesh cannot please God" (Romans 8:5–8).

Until your children realize salvation is as easy as ABC (admit, believe, and confess) but is deep and more meaningful than anything in the world, they still are dead in sin—but they can be made alive in Christ! "As for you, you were dead in your transgressions and sins in which you used to live when you followed the ways of this world and of the ruler of the kingdom of the air, the Spirit who is now at work in those who are disobedient" (Ephesians 2:1–2). Paul admonishes Timothy to "always be sober-minded, endure suffering, do the work of an evangelist, fulfill your ministry" (2 Timothy 4:5).

Graduation from Suffering

As we continue to be students of God's Word, may we continue to teach our children. It is possible to lose heart over problems. Not to underscore the physical separation of death and loss, but anxiety never changes your reality. On the contrary, stress compromises your present and robs your future.

My years as a hospice crisis care nurse could not have been a better training ground for terminal illness and death. There are some answers we may never get in this broken world. Listen to the comforting words of Paul: "For I consider that the sufferings of this present time are not worth comparing with the glory that is to be revealed to us" (Romans 8:18).

If you lose your child, don't lose your mind. If your child is on the streets, don't lose your head. If your child has a disability, don't lose your sanity. If you lose your teeth, do not lose your identity. If you lose your loved ones, do not lose your life. If you lose your child, do not lose your faith. If you get kicked out of the Church, your eternity is guaranteed!

You will never graduate from problems, but with the practical application of God's Word, you can grow and have a different perspective. Most of the issues you have are magnified by the illusion that life should be ideal and trouble-free. Your child's ugly past and the ongoing detour cannot survive in your heavy presence! We keep fighting from victory from the victory obtained at the cross, the death and resurrection of Jesus Christ. Apostle Paul writes, "But thanks be to God, who gives us the victory through our Lord Jesus Christ" (1 Corinthians 15:57).

Focus on the present! Each day has its challenges! Whatever you are going through, be present. Focus on your now. Do not imagine that the situation should have been different. You were intended to go through that test victoriously.

Victory lies in the stillness of now. You know that God is entirely in control of your child's life. In the great circle of life, there is no permanence. Everything but God is vanity, a passing cloud. Learn to surrender to his will every moment you live. Be sober, irrespective of what your long, unending journey looks like. Be calm despite your circumstances. It is possible to have joy in the midst of the detours by meditating on Philippians 4:7–8, "And the peace of God, which surpasses all understanding, will guard your hearts and your minds in Christ Jesus. Finally, brothers, whatever is true, whatever is honorable, whatever is just, whatever is pure, whatever is lovely, whatever is commendable, if there is any excellence, if there is anything worthy of praise, think about these things."

Tears and Joy

Happiness is temporary. It is not a factor in the painful years of parenting, but joy is drawn from within. "Then he said to them, 'Go your way. Eat the fat and drink sweet wine and send portions to anyone who has nothing ready, for this day is holy to our Lord. And do not be grieved, for the joy of the LORD is your strength'" (Nehemiah 8:10). The pathway to this joy can be acquired by practical tips. Have they worked for me? Absolutely

The family requires stability to count on. Parents must project confidence in worst-case scenarios like we face today. However, that does not hinder us from privately staying tethered to the reality that we are entirely dependent on God.

Yet as you go, keep the oxygen of God's supernatural supply flowing with your every breath. In his Spirit power, you can find the strength to parent, as Jehoshaphat did next. "He set out. He stood up. He spoke" (2 Chronicles 20:20). Set out in faith that God is with you. Stand up on the Rock of Ages, Jesus Christ.

Jehoshaphat did one final thing before heading into the battle: he praised God. The king thanked God for the victory God had promised. That is an assurance it is possible to be joyful in trials, even in the detours!

Do not isolate, but insulate

Do you know why so many parents are getting it wrong when raising strong, confident, and Christ-centered young adults?

It is not what you think! Most people think the key to raising young adults who love Jesus, make good decisions, and are heading in the right direction with their lives is about protecting them from all the bad stuff in the world. You cannot isolate them, but you can insulate them in the truth and appropriate disciplines. Our prayer should be in line with the words of Jesus in the gospel of John: "I do not ask that you take them out of the world, but that you keep them from the evil one" (John 17:15). The truth is if you plan to shelter your child until adulthood, you are merely delaying the inevitable. It is like sticking your fingers into the holes of a sinking boat and hoping you can row to shore before you sink.

What if there was a better way? As earlier discussed, what if you could walk shoulder to shoulder with your children through their younger years and raise them to view the world through a gospel lens? You can insulate them in his Word, but you cannot isolate them. They will make choices, good and bad, and each is a teachable moment for them—and you as well. The only avenue for them to navigate issues is with a biblical worldview that is unshakable. It is possible to mold and influence them.

We believe they can, but it is going to take parents who are willing to shift from the way things used to be back in the days to the way things needs to be, along with a robust theological foundation.

Let Loose the Lion

Charles Spurgeon, the nineteenth-century Baptist preacher, once said if you let loose the lion, the lion will defend itself and needs no defense. All that the king of the jungle needs, according to Spurgeon, is to get out of the cage! If the Word of God is preached, it will take care of itself. If a lion is let loose, who can dare encounter him? The good news is the reality of the gospel needs to go in our children's lives like a lion in its majesty! According to Paul, "This is good and pleasing in the sight God our Savior, who desires all people to be saved and to come to a knowledge of the truth" (1 Timothy 2:3–4).

The First and Top Evangelist

As discussed earlier, in your ambassadorial role, you are first and top evangelist to your children. Teach your children the scriptures and demonstrate them by your lifestyle. Tell them you needed a Savior too! Show them their need for a Savior and point them to Jesus Christ as the only one who can save them from their sins.

This command is loud and clear, as written in the book of Deuteronomy.

> The LORD our God, the LORD is one. You shall love the LORD your God with all your heart and

> with all your soul and with all your might. And these words that I command you today shall be on your heart. You shall teach them diligently to your children, and shall talk of them when you sit in your house, and when you walk by the way, and when you lie down, and when you rise. You shall bind them as a sign on your hand, and they shall be as frontlets between your eyes. You shall write them on the doorposts of your house and on your gates. (Deuteronomy 6:6–9)

Parents, as you speak and teach the Word of God, whether it be in the kitchen, on your small runs to the grocery store, on a long road trip, or in little verses on your bathroom mirror, just do it! The Lord himself will do good work in our child! As the lion clears its own path and eases itself of all adversaries, so is the Word of God to your child.

"But I have tried. The more I speak about God's Word, the more my child rebels. And my child questions with an attitude, asking, 'Must it always be about this Jesus? Must it always be a lesson?'"

Take caution not to force, coerce, or manipulate your children into a profession of faith, which could be false, out of fear and parental pressure. They should know and develop a relationship with God, loving him and worshipping him. Eventually it become a lifestyle. If you teach your children about t their sins and the need for the Savior, and if you model the same teaching, the Lord will turn their hearts to himself at his own time. Yes, at his time, as is his desire.

Parents, what is that too hard for the Lord? Absolutely nothing! No adversary, no detour encountered by the lion can survive! Let the lion loose!

Benchmark Parenting

Are you battle weary? We could be identical twins in some ways! There is a conspicuous trend of a prayer journal saved on a hard drive for more than a decade. For years I asked God for his direction for my children, and for clarity in times of confusion and uninvited detours. With major career, education, and family transitions, I needed a burning bush experience, an intravenous infusion of God's power and presence.

But Satan, the enemy, was busy in the battlefield of my mind, whispering, "You are not good enough, wife. Do more to be a better parent. Do more to be a perfect healthcare worker." He told me many more lies!

But there is a temptation to execute my parental duties with a prescription—or is it legalism? In my fear of my children making mistakes and making bad choices, I did not give them the freedom to make mistakes, the freedom to be different, the freedom to be candid or vulnerable. That is a flat-out, failure-filled parental burden! It is benchmark parenting at its worst! But let us fall back to the burden bearer that guides and shepherds the heart of your child well. His name is Jesus!

We cannot shy away from him in every aspect of our lives, or be offended. "And blessed is he who is not offended because of me" (Matthew 11:6). Jesus gives an invitation, and the invitation is an ordinary coming to see and hear him preach to multitudes. It is believing in him, submitting to his grace and authority, and putting your faith and trust in him. Trust in His righteousness and salvation, and in return get relief from your distressed mind.

Dear parents, you are the righteousness of God. Your sins have been washed away. Your children will make their choices. No guilt! No shame! You are redeemed by the Son of God. Remember that your sins are washed away, and you are made clean because Christ gave his own body as a gift to God. He did this once for all time, and you will make it by his grace and power.

He gives an invitation to you to rest all the parental and family exhaustion and condemnation in the gospel of Matthew: "Come to me, all who labor and are heavy laden" (Matthew 11:28a). Are you exhausted from trying to control your child's life? Are you emotionally and mentally exhausted from using your strength, and now you are at your wits' ends, and your parental efforts are futile? "And I will give you rest" (Matthew 11:28b). Jesus promises rest.

King David shares his experience: "The LORD preserves the simple; when I was brought low, he saved me. Return, O my soul, to your rest; for the LORD has dealt bountifully with you" (Psalm 116:6–7).

Under his troubles, David was supported by God and was brought low in the depth of his misery. He got the help to pray in his distress and to wait patiently in his shattered faith, and indeed he was able to hope for the best and bear the worst.

David chose to live, delighting in God, and was not agitated with fear of the unknown. He had the assurance of God dealing with him kindly. "For the LORD has dealt bountifully with you" (Psalm 116:7).

Rest

Rest does not come easy while carrying all the parental baggage. It is work in process! Jesus is our rest and is the secret spiritual weapon of grace parenting. Jesus is our rock. The joy we have in Jesus does not mean we will not have problems; rather, we have a Savior who intercedes and a loving Father who loves us unconditionally. As our faith family lead pastor, David Welch, once stated in his weekly impactful messages, "God loves you because He loves you; not even a million failures could stop him." In Paul's and Silas's same footsteps, when the foundations are shaken, hold on to the more significant rock. This is spiritual rest, refreshment, rejuvenation, and relief for your weary parental soul. Remember that the enemy knows the one weapon and first line of defense is vital, and he will do anything to distract you. Do no not let him!

Grace Reigns

Parenting in the power and influence of God's grace is an essential. When we disobey God, there are consequences, but when we obey and walk with God, he blesses us with his peace, joy, and bliss. The same grace is accorded to our children. Peter states, "But grow in the grace and knowledge of our Lord and Savior Jesus Christ. To him be the glory both now and to the day of eternity. Amen" (2 Peter 3:18). No matter the outcome in the journey, your parenting will be more comfortable with God's grace and steadfast love, and with an eternal reward!

Unconditional Love

You are as a parent and a mediator of Christ's love, but it has been a challenge, another work in progress. How about being a mediator of peace? When experiences and difficulties take preeminence, we put our faith in God himself, rest the welfare of our souls, and increase our faith in God.

The Lord told Hosea, "And the LORD said to me, "Go again, love a woman who is loved by another man and is an adulteress, even as the LORD loves the children of Israel, though they turn to other gods and love cakes of raisins" (Hosea 3:1).

"Just as Christ loves the church, we are to love others, Husbands love your wives as Christ loved the church" (Ephesians 5:25). Many children have made bad choices, but in dire circumstances, we are to love them unconditionally. Can parents bring curses or blessings on their children? One of my sons asked me, "Mom, does God honor the curse of a parent?" It is an interesting lengthy topic, and the long and short of it is a believer in Christ cannot be cursed, but life choices have consequences.

Don't we all appreciate positive affirmations in our careers and relationships? In the same way your words as a parent have a great impact on your child, they can be hurtful words, causing great pain and longtime consequences. Or they can cause loving affirmations, compassion, care and guidance. Being a parent is a God-given authority over your children, and the courses of their lives can be determined by the power of your words!

Most parents are well meaning and bless children with their words, however a slip of the tongue can cause lasting harm and wounds. No harm in emphasis of God's Word: Proverbs 18:21 states, "Death and life are in the power of the tongue and those who love it will eat its fruits."

It is in the nitty-gritty details of life that we get our prayers answered and desires fulfilled. When we change our words, we change our children's world and destinies!

Wounded Healers

It is always good to know that even those who seem to have it together have their ups and downs. That is a beautifully written description of life.

When we pass through trials, God pours to us his love and comforts us to stream the same comfort to hurting parents. Paul says we are charged to comfort others as Christ has settled us, as written by Apostle Paul in Corinthians: "Blessed be the God and Father of our Lord Jesus Christ, the Father of mercies and God of all comfort, who comforts us in all our affliction, so that we may be able to comfort those who are in any affliction, with the comfort with which we ourselves are comforted by God. For as we share abundantly in Christ's sufferings, so through Christ we share abundantly in comfort too" (2 Corinthians 1:3–5).

I am eternally grateful to many "able ministers" (2 Corinthians 3:6) who stand in the gap of hurting mothers and children, the women and men who wail to God on your behalf of our children. They are jewels in our Father's vineyard. Our calling is a comfort chain, as Apostle Paul states: "I wrote this very thing so that when I came, I would not have pain from those who ought to give me joy, because I am confident about all of you that my joy will also be yours" (2 Corinthians 2:3).

I join hurting mothers in prayers, saying to them, "I was where you are; that was my experience and worse. But God!" According to Hosea, God says, "I am the God who opens a door of hope" (Hosea 2:15). How comforting to meet an overcomer and someone who has gone through the same and worse trials, and who says, "I have gone through the same trials, and I met a God who opened the door of hope."

Just like the days of Aaron ad Hur, Exodus records, "But Moses's hands grew weary, so they took a stone and put it under him, and he sat on it, while Aaron and Hur held up his hands one on one side, the other on the other side. So his hands were steady until the going down of the sun" (Exodus 17:12–13).

There is a famous saying: "God's grace can save souls without our preaching, but our preaching cannot save them without God's grace, and that grace must be sought by prayer." Each one of us has a unique personal parental journey. Remember, I am not an expert but simply a veteran on this journey!

6

GPS Signal Lost, Navigation Rerouting

> Strength is not measured by what you avoided
> but by what you faced and survived in life.
> —Anonymous

Let me pause and approach this critical issue of trial by Fire from another perspective. I grew up at the slopes of Mount Kenya. At the young age of about eight, I had a picture of God: he lived above the clouds up, above the mountain and sky. Every time my praying grandmother would narrate stories of Paul and Timothy, her favorite Bible characters, she would also point at the heavens above, and that cemented my view of God. This picture of God grew with me, and I was always in awe of a God who sits in a throne room in the sky and watches the affairs of humans, his creation—and occasionally strikes like thunder!

King David could have known nothing about Mount Kenya but was aware of where to turn to in times of danger. This painted a literal picture of the God who resides in skies. The psalmist wrote, "I will lift my eyes to the hills, from where comes my help? My help comes from the Lord, who made heaven and earth" (Psalm 121:1). More emphasis on my mother tongue,

Kikuyu, made it more real and memorable regarding God's image.

It was bringing the principle of spiritual warfare closer to home. How does this apply to you and me as parents? Could it be that our Father, who is in heaven, allows parents and children to struggle in order to keep us healthy? I do not believe that to be true.

You have not had a mission executed without a notice! My wake-up call was issued without warning. Despite knowing Christ and serving Him, the trials knocked at my doorstep. I lived a defeated life, trying to fix my parental struggles, and I tried and failed repeatedly. My life was contrary to what the life of a believer in the Lord Jesus reflects!

I was plagued with unimaginable thoughts of guilt, anxiety, and compulsions, and my anger was contrary to the Word of God. You ask, "Is it not okay to be angry when the GPS signal is lost and unexpected detour is head on your journey ?

War Exposed

Do you realize there is a raging war an unseen around you? It is a spiritual war. Yes, an unseen war!Today,the GPS is a great tool, the real deal for for guidance in most journeys,however detours causes the signal to be lost while navigating.

War is being raged in the heavens, and God is calling you as a parent to wake up to it.How do you navigate? How about you stop and restart the navigation?

Spiritual Warfare

I did not recognize a current war around me as a mother and parent for a long time. Did I say I had heard of the fight, or were there simply rumors of parenting war? What about what you are going through? "All these are the beginnings of sorrows"

(Isaiah 66:6). It is as if he said these are only the first pangs and are nothing to that calamity awaiting. You are asking, "Can a loving God take you through war?"

I remember with fondness stories from my late mother as she sat at the kitchen fireplace. She talked about the Mau Mau rebellion, a nationalist movement that advocated violent resistance to being a British colony. It was marked with bloody, widespread, oppressive violence. My mother recalled the aftermath and clearly stated she detested war and would not wish war on anyone, even her worst enemies.

In further reading, I was interested in learning about global wars. Certain journals of interest recognized that the study of *war in history is* more than merely studying conflict; it embraces war in broader aspects—economic, social, political, and military. Wars have lasting direct and indirect consequences. As parents, we may not be experiencing the physical war, but a spiritual war is equally bad.

Rerouting Handbook for the 21st Century Parent

Why has your parental journey turned out to be a nightmare? You are probably asking, "Is this my daily walk?" What causes loss of the GPS signal in your's child's life ? It's the unseen battle, waging war. Only God can open your spiritual eyes to see and understand the physical manifestations. The attacks of the evil one are real, but how do you fix a lost GPS signal?

Through prayer and his Word, you can get a spiritual awakening and awareness, as written by Apostle Paul: "Finally, be strong in the Lord and in the strength of his might. Put on the whole armor of God, that you may be able to stand against the schemes of the devil. For we do not wrestle against flesh and blood, but against the rulers, against the authorities, against the cosmic powers over this present darkness, against the spiritual forces of evil in the heavenly places" (Ephesians

6:10–12). No doubt the decisions and battles are real in the spiritual world, impacting parenting journeys and lives.

You must let God's Word become the words you park your mind and heart on. You must let God's Word become the words of your story over your child.Though the GPS signal is lost His word remains the rerouting handbook.When you get into the fight through His Word and let God be God, you gain inner peace.

Jesus Invition To A Narrow Path

When Jesus said, "Follow me" (Matthew 4:19) to his disciples, he invited them to walk the same narrow path—the same as you on your parenting journey. Today seems to have twists and turns, too many detours and storms. Your daughter has eloped. You are dealing with a troubled teen. Your child is a victim of cyberbullying around the clock and is experiencing isolation, depression, or even suicidal thoughts. Alcohol and drugs are at your doorstep. No matter your family status, I have good news to share: the liberating truth that feeling does not mean being forsaken, but God will never leave us or forsake us. There is assured victory in the warfare. God allows us to feel, but his purpose will be fulfilled. Jesus is a good example of utter dependance upon God, with the feeling of despair and weight of the sin of the world, yet he triumphed over the grave even after he felt forsaken. Our hope is in the promises of God of deliverance and hope of resurrection.

Jesus is extending the same invitation to walk the narrow road less traveled. It does not accommodate or allow worldliness. It leads to God's blessings, and the other wide road leads to destruction. We can make that choice as parents and more so our children as well.

Jesus speaks of this: "For the gate is narrow and the way is hard that leads to life, and those who find it are few" (Matthew 7:14). That is an affirmation that every choice has a consequence.

Get into the Fight

No doubt as a parent, you can quickly grow tired along the way, as though in a lion's den parenting season. But how about shifting the gear and thinking of the spiritual war already won? Apostle Paul reminds us of our victory and spiritual blessing in Christ when he writes, "Blessed be the God and Father of our Lord Jesus Christ, who has blessed us in Christ with every spiritual blessing in the heavenly places" (Ephesians 1:3). With this assurance, we can no longer live in defeat but can confidently parent well with the assured blessings.

Balance Feedback and Boundaries

The challenges of detours calls for much-needed prayer, counseling, wisdom, and homeostasis. There is need to seek stability and equilibrium, and each family member is functioning to keep the family unit in balance even when it does not favor everyone. When friends visit, *all is well* to reduce fights between a parent and a child, to keep the family's sanity and peace.

Family therapy is a useful intervention to create healthy boundaries and accountability. In times of emotional turmoil, burden bearers come in handy to pray and declare God's promises. "From the fruit of a man's mouth his stomach is satisfied; he is satisfied by the yield of his lips" (Proverbs 18:21). There is power in the tongue. It is possible to agree and declare no negative effects of a detour can have an effect on the entire family.

Furthermore, this day I am forever grateful and can only echo the words of Apostle John: "I have no greater joy than to hear that my children are walking in the truth" (3 John 1:4). Individual therapy was useful in affirming a child's decision to accept a life transformation. It reinforced the importance of establishing an identity in Christ.

Wake up to the Fight

I am not sure about you, but during my faith walk, I thought following Christ was all about rules, regulations, and rituals. Little did I know that in his presence, there is fullness of joy in the middle of an unseen war. With much prayer, reading, study, meditating on the Word, and fellowship with other believers, I woke up to the spiritual world reality. What was happening in my family was a manifestation of what was happening in the spiritual realm.

The battle was no longer fixed, or against one member of the family. I realized the gift was a conduit for the spiritual warfare in heavenly places. Was that easy? No. When my flesh waged war against the spirit and wanted to do battle with the physical, the mother-child was sour because I could not comprehend the actions. I felt betrayed and let down, and the family image was destroyed. I wanted my child to get to normalcy and stop the behavior, but to no avail. Doing that was like a police officer watching the television in his living room and pulling a gun on a criminal he sees on a reality television show. If the officer shoots at the television, he will merely add more problems to the mess that is already going on.

It is a momentarily right moment with no accomplishment or solution, like jumping from the pan and into the fire. Does this mean spending a day of prayer in the war room? No, but the morning prayers engaging in the spiritual realm gave me more confidence and power to tackle the destructive detour.

The realization of spiritual warfare victory and development in detours lit a spiritual bulb and brought peace and spiritual victory. I no longer settled for microwave prayer answers or easy fixes, and I submitted myself to the Lord as I asked him to mold the clay as a potter does. His Word, worship, and prayer were essential in that season in my parenting journey.

Spiritual Awareness and Sensitivity

Some questions to you: Who and what is your image of God? When in danger, in the fiery furnace of parenting, where do you seek help? You may be looking at your current situation in your daughter and son and see no hope.

The psalmist encourages you to seek protection in the Lord, who is a present help in times of trouble. His Word offers assurance that God is aware of the people and circumstances that threaten your livelihood and make attacks on your children. Blessed assurance is promised!

However, how is this possible with all the turmoil and emotional pain while your child is taking a downward spiral? I have found it easier to trust him with my children and parenting journey because he is an able God and I am not. Moreover, given his promises as written in the book of Job, you and I have not experienced even a quarter of his parental nightmare, yet he could still be optimistic enough to say, "For I know that my Redeemer lives, and at last he will stand upon the earth. And after my skin has been thus destroyed, yet in my flesh, I shall see God, whom I shall see for myself and my eyes shall behold and not another. My heart faints within me!" (Job 19:25). We are capable of overcoming the hurt and frustration of a wayward child.

The Lord Fights for You

The future was full of promise. School lay behind him. His career and his bride-to-be stood before him. However, then came the terminal diagnosis of cancer. Going back could not save him. Going forward seemed impossible. He was terrified. Why had God led him to this seeming dead-end?

The Israelites found themselves in a similar place of fear. God was leading them from slavery in Egypt to the Promised Land. However, then Pharaoh summoned his army and pursued the Israelites to the Red Sea. With the sea in front of them and Pharaoh's army behind them, the Israelites were terrified. That night, the Lord drove the Red Sea back, divided its waters to save the Israelites, and drowned their pursuers. When the Israelites saw God's might in action, they honored the Lord and put their faith in him.

God still answers our fears. Doctors gave that graduate a grim prognosis. There was nothing he could do but quiet his heart and go forward. Furthermore, the Lord fought for him. Within months, his cancer was gone. He has been happily married for seventeen years and is blessed with two daughters.

The Lord also fights for you. He already has. Jesus endured the cross and overcame its curse for you. By his resurrection, he opened a way through death to the Promised Land of heaven for you.

When there is no way back and there seems to be no way forward, remember to honor the Lord by trusting him. There is hope, as further stated by Job: "For there is hope for a tree: If it is cut down, it will sprout again, and its new shoots will not cease. Though Its roots may grow old in the earth, and its stump die in the soil, yet at the scent of water, it will bud and put out branches like a young plant" (Job 14:7–9).

Pruning and Praising Him in the Waiting

The waiting season to see the manifestation of God's Word was my biggest challenge, praying day and night with no change. I must confess that we call it "microwavable prayers," praying according to my will instead of praying and believing God for the manifestation of His Word. My patience was tested more than any other season in my parenting journey. The stern test was my faith and willingness to rest on God's promises. Together with that, the fruit of the spirit did not reflect well in the waiting.

I reinforced my trust and commitment to God, even when

I had every reason not to trust him and nothing made sense. Praying time and time again with no sign of change, my mind took me on a road trip of thoughts that God might be silent. The most challenging thing was not knowing when God would answer prayers, but the lack of a sign was emotionally draining.

I can only imagine your emotional pain and trusting God for so many years make you took the wrong path, or you have a terminal illness. Maybe it is a situation your child is going through.

As a parent, you have been on your knees, wailing and asking for God's intervention, yet it seems your child is getting worse. Yes, it is frustrating, the wait is long, it is agonizing, and you are currently battling with depression and anxiety. You are fighting so hard so you can have peace that surpasses all understanding.

And yet at times, you'll find yourself in tears, and all you can say is, "When, God?" The longer you have to wait, the more you realize that there is absolutely nothing you can do to manipulate God's timing. You get to a point where he starts to make you know that you are blessed not because of what you have or what you do not have, but because he is still there with you even on nights when the pain is unbearable and you cry yourself to sleep.

It is time for you to cling to his promises. The Lord has exemplary commitment over you and the seed of your womb, and you cannot give up on God. The only choice you have is to keep trusting him, keep the faith, and do not let the devil make you believe the lie that God is never going to transform your child and restore your peace.

You Have One Enemy

Right now is the perfect time to stop and pay attention to what you are focusing on this moment. Are you rehashing hurtful moments with your child, or words that your adult child has said? Or are you filling your thoughts with God's healing words? You must set your mind and your heart on things above by choosing to remember God's words, repeat God's words, and believe God's words about your child.

Get in the Fight

For a long time, I was plagued with emotional pain, anxiety, and depression over my child's outcome. I had a realization that God has already given his children everything needed to parent in victory. Through the life, death, and resurrection of Jesus, we have parenting assurance with grace and success.

You have to believe that Jesus Christ's victory is our victory by connecting what you see and experience in your parenting journey with what God has promised concerning your child to the invisible spiritual world, a spiritual Warfare!

As a believer in the Lord Jesus Christ, parenting with challenges requires an understanding that there is a need for your spiritual eyes to be open to the spiritual reality in the physical. You and I need Ephesian 6:13-19 stated by Apostle Paul to reroue our parental navigation system.

"Therefore take up the whole armor of God, that you may be able to withstand in the evil day, and having done all, to stand firm. Stand therefore, having fastened on the belt of truth and having put on the breastplate of righteousness and as shoes for your feet, having put on the readiness given bythe gospel of peace. In all circumstances take up the shield of Faith, with which you can extinguish all the flaming darts of the evil one: and take the helmet ofsalvation, and the sword of the spirit, which is the word of God, praying at all times, in the spirit with allprayer and supplication. To that end keep alert with all perseverance, making supplication for all the saints, and also for me, that words may be given to me in opening my mouth bodly to proclaim the mystery of the gospel.

You know Satan is a deceiver and traps you as a parent

to see your child as the main problem. No doubt they make wrong choices and suffer the consequences, but there is grace available to those who fear the Lord and turn to Jesus as Lord and Savior. A sure hope for spiritual GPS restored ! Psalm 9:10 "The fear of the Lord is beginning of wisdom."

7

From Faith To Faith

Using God's truth as your fighting words will not change what you see, but absolutely will change how you see it.

—Lysa Terkeust

In my parenting journey, I have had unreal expectations of my children my pain and emotions were contradictory to the confession of God's unfailing promises. I tried to control the outcomes with my five senses, making the situation worse.

Baking with my teenage daughter as I write this book is another bonding mother-daughter moment. Watching her get the recipes to the icing of the gluten-free pumpkin cake or sometimes indulging on a simple pound cake warms my heart! The oven at times gets hot, and the recipes may get messy, but knowing we can have our cake and eat it makes it better. The outcome is always exciting!

Isn't part of our parental journey sometimes like that for you? The journey is sometimes likened to being in broil mode. We wish to have the icing of the cake but forget it is a process .A journey started in Faith endured through faith,passing on your faith one generation to another similar to what King David points in his best praise Psalm 145:4 "One generation shall commend your works to another, and shall declare your mighty acts."

I can testify for myself and from seeing thousands of parental interactions that we are very attached to our children's outcomes, from their first cries to their developmental growth, grades, educational pursuits, choice of partners, and every aspect of their lives. We say we trust God, but our response to their storms when it seems the world is crippling us is a test of our faith in God. The oven of our journey gets unbearable at times Faith is measured by what you do, not by what you say you are going to do.

Children's Character

God's promises offer comfort to parents who are facing seemingly senseless tragedy and overwhelmed in their parenting journey. The pain is so real and undeniable, but by faith, you trust God to do what he has promised. In my anger, I lecture, I yell, and all seems go to deaf ears. But as author Paul Tripp writes in his book *Parenting*, "Not all of the wrong your children do is a direct rebellion to authority ;much of the wrong is the result of a lack of character." I have struggled with some of my children's character, and my faith is tried and tested in moments like this. God's grace not only favors us but powers us to communicate and understand the situation.

Our children's defiance comes from within their hearts and is displayed in their choices. A broader discussion on what rules a child's heart will occur later.

Do you not praise God when your children are successful according to the worldly standards? You are faced with sudden tragedies or unexpected parental outcomes, such as an adult child making choices contrary to your belief and expectation. They turn to a different sexual orientation, substance abuse, prostitution, poor choices of relationships, a high temper, disobedience, suicide, and many other poor choices. They get entangled in sin. The natural question is why? You question God, don't you? "Lord, why did this happen to my child, and why now?" In part, some of these questions were answered in previous chapters.

We must lean on faith when the unthinkable happens, and we must gain strength amid the storm. You are not alone, and Job struggled with the same question of why. "If I have sinned, what do I do to you, you watcher of mankind ? Why have you made me your mark? Why have I become a burden to you? Why do you not pardon my transgression and take away my iniquity? For now I shall lie in the earth; you will seek me, but I shall not be" (Job 7:20–21). To Job, that season did not make sense, but eventually he realized God's excellent glory and grace in his suffering and the tragedy of his children. How can one count it all as joy with a shattered faith?

Faith in God Brings Joy

The only real constant and the only thing that truly makes any sense in your life is the Word of God, prayer, and faith in him alone. Choosing joy in parenting is not the absence of storms. There are hurricanes, cyclones, tornadoes, floods, and fires, but through them all, the Lord requires you and me to trust him and exercise our faith. Prophet Isaiah tells of the only Savior and the pleasant help. "But now, thus says the Lord, he who created you, O Jacob, he who formed you, O Israel: Fear not, for I have redeemed you; I have called you by name; you are mine. When you pass through the waters, I will be with you; and through the rivers, they will not overwhelm you. When you walk through the fire, you will not be burned; and the flame shall not consume you" (Isaiah 43:1–2).

You'll learn how joy is the settled assurance that God is in control of all the details of your life and your child's life, the quiet confidence that ultimately everything will be okay, and the determined choice to praise him in all things even when the evidence tells you otherwise.

The Hall of Faithfulness

My fellow parents, get ready—there's a train coming. You don't need any ticket or luggage; you simply get on board. All you need is faith to hear the gallons of diesel humming. Thank the Lord for the gift of the womb. Faith is all you need, as Apostle Paul declared in Hebrews 10:38a, "But my righteous one shall live by faith."

I thought I could do a sprint through my parenting, but I was reminded to rely upon the obedience of parenting by Faith in the stormy race even when I did not understand. Now is my time and yours to run the parenting race with endurance and faith, knowing we are surrounded by a great cloud of witnesses.

Some Bible commands may seem difficult, unreasonable, or impossible. Impossible is not found in Him, and He knows more than you do what is best for you and your child. Could the distractions be a test of your faith? Do you trust God, or do you trust your feelings? Trust the Word and not the world!

While growing up, I stubbornly questioned some of my parents' commands that seemed difficult, and when I dared to ask, "Why should I do this?" the answer was, "Because I said it!" Looking back at those things, they make sense now, and I admire the wisdom of my parents.

I look back at the life of these great people, such as Abraham, Noah, and many more! Just like God did with them, He may command you to do things you may not comprehend or things that do not make sense. Believe when you do not see it and obey when you do not understand. That's faith!

You might be afraid that God might not come through for you and your child. I have wrestled with that feeling! When things get tough, I am tempted to rally more of my strength rather than rely on God's power. It is easy to say I trust God with my mouth, but in reality I get overwhelmed trying to fix and control things. I get stressed out, overly emotional, and more distant from God. My trust in God becomes nothing but a statement I feel I should say, but it is not what I am living out.

The five senses of hearing, seeing, tasting, touching, and smelling come to most of us naturally. To the believer of Jesus Christ, there is a sixth sense: faith, to function in the spiritual realm.

Our ambassadorial parenting is to please God, as it is written in Hebrews: "Now without faith, it is impossible to be well-pleasing to him, for he who comes to God must believe that he exists and that he is a rewarder of those who seek him" *(Hebrews 11:6).*

The enemy, Satan, wants you to doubt so you can miss the best. Listen and believe God, who can never lie. Come to Him with faith, not fear. Doubts, anxiety, and discouragement will keep you from receiving your miracles. Fight fear and distrust, focus on God's promise, and *feed your faith. As* the psalmist says, "Your testimonies are my comfort, Your testimonies are my delight; they are my counselors" (Psalm 119:24).

Faith Is a Gift

Faith is not something that has to be contrived or worked up. Scripture tells us that everyone has been given a measure of faith. It also says that faith grows or comes as we hear the Word of God. That is why it is essential to stay connected to a Bible-based church where the Word of God is being taught. It is why we need to make time every day to read and study his Word, because that is how we feed our faith. The more we know his Word, the more we understand that God is good, and he rewards the people who seek after him.

The Foundation

Faith is the basis of everything. We believe and then receive, as noted in example scriptures.

> By faith Enoch was taken up so that he should not see death, and he was not found, because God had taken him. Now before he was taken he was commended as having pleased God. And without faith it is impossible to please him, for whoever would draw near to God must believe that he exists and that he rewards those who seek him. By faith Noah, being warned by God concerning events as yet unseen, in reverent fear constructed an ark for the saving of his household. By this he condemned the world and became an heir of the righteousness that comes by faith. (Hebrews 11:5–7)

Upheld with Outstretched Arms

In the last chapter, we discussed the nature of a believer's war. Paul explains how God chose to use the weak things of the world to shame those that rely on their physical strength, whether it be man's military might, the political mechanisms of human government, the social influences, or parental wisdom. He wrote in 1 Corinthians 1:27, "But God has chosen the foolish things of the world to shame the wise, and God has chosen the weak things of the world to shame the things which are strong."

As a parent, I used my authority to pick and choose what worked in my parenting journey, but then I realized God's Word is not a buffet where you pick and choose scriptures to suit your parenting journey, even when the journey gets tough. In my acquired knowledge and self-assurance in the ways I was raised, self-confidence was a recipe for parental disaster. God has chosen the foolish things of the world to shame those who are wise in their own eyes.

How does God's message using the world's foolish things to shame the wise, and how does it apply to your parenting journey? It brings to nothing the wisdom of the wise. It silences the philosopher's brilliance and dismantles the strength of brutish men who are mighty in their own eyes.

God has ordained that eternal parental wisdom comes from preaching the death, burial, and resurrection of Jesus Christ. He alone has the power and knowledge. Although God's way of salvation is foolishness in the eyes of the world, you have to recognize that the only path to eternal salvation and everlasting life comes from faith in the death, burial, and resurrection of the Lord Jesus Christ.

Unsanctified common sense is of no consequence in the eternal plan of God and day-to-day parental journey. After the total surrender, I turned my values as a mother, and my wisdom and power were utterly demolished by the knowledge and power of God so that I may never boast in my strength or power.

Your boasting in your children must only come from the Lord Jesus and him being crucified, for he is the personification of God's wisdom and strength. Wisdom comes from God alone, and his sufficient power is to be found only in the person and work of Jesus Christ, the incarnate Son of God.

Through it all, the glorious works of God become manifest. Just like Job, the grace and glory of God is possible through suffering. "Then Job replied to the Lord: 'I know that you can do all things; no purpose of yours can be thwarted. You asked, "Who is this that obscures my plans without knowledge?" Surely I spoke of things I did not understand, things too wonderful for me to know. You said, "Listen now, and I will speak; I will question you, and you shall answer me." My ears had heard of you, but now my eyes have seen you. Therefore I despise myself and repent in dust and ashes'" (Job 42:1–6).

God's Word is the truth, and his truth says in Proverbs 11:21, "Be assured, an evil person will not go unpunished, but the offspring of the righteous will be delivered." All the parents, especially mothers, shall say, Let it be! God knows your children, and they are lavishly loved by him no matter what they have done. The enemy may take you on a guilt trip that has resulted in their poor behavior, but the unwavering truth of his Word remains. God loves your children too much to not answer your prayers, but they will be answered at his time and in his plans. Your wailing, the morning glory, the lunch hour prayers, and the evening prayers are not in vain!

You will be molded and shaped into his image, and when you know God as Lord, then you discover who you are in him. There was a time when I would say yes and amen to this statement made by preachers without much reasoning. But the more I matured by feeding his Word constantly, the more I realized I have not discovered God. I can only submit in agreement with him about who he is and who I am in him. The idea of my discovery led to a better understanding, and I am complete in him, Yes, I am forgiven by grace and love unimaginable! He has put my broken pieces together again, and I praise God every day. "For we walk by faith and not by sight" (2 Corinthians 5:7).

There is perhaps no better illustration of this truth of God's words on faith than the written piece by Molly, a patient in palliative care with a terminal illness.

> I have confidence, hope, and assurance about what I do not see because I know my right leg won't let me down. The doctor says my organs have failed! I have less than six months to exit this earthly tent!
>
> I have put my confidence in the things I can't do with my right leg, and I also believe that God is in control of my life. And how can I have this confidence, hope, and assurance? Because it has been my life experience. God has never let me down. He's always been faithful in every storm, every need, every heartbreak. He's carried me, held me, guided me, comforted me, as well as blessed me, moved mountains for me, and even taken down a few giants for me. Why would this

chronic disease diabetes be any different? Do I know what's ahead for me? No, but I'm confident that God is right there with me, and He is faithful even though I can't walk, as my right leg is amputated, with unbearable pain depending on my left leg—it's dependable, and I can trust it.

I will continue to use the wheelchair proudly and continue to walk by faith and not by sight.

How about you? Your struggles may not look like mine, but probably just as difficult to maneuver. I can assure you, walking by Faith and confidence in God is far better than walking by what you see going on around you. So, hey, Get out your clutches and let's walk by faith today. And what is Faith? Hebrews 11:1 says this: "Now faith is confidence in what we hope for and assurance about what we do not see."

God safely takes us through the hardest of times of our parenting. Once we reach the other side, it comes to us that with only our sight and effort, we wouldn't have gotten any further than where we started from, as stated in Exodus 18:18, "You and the people with you will certainly wear yourselves out, for the thing is too heavy for you. You are not able to do it alone!" These words came at the perfect time, reminding me that being confident that God is in control is always the pathway to peace, especially when nothing made sense in my disappointing times of parenting and walk with God.

Sense of Purpose: God Does Not Waste an Opportunity

Sometimes when we are in trouble, we do not dare to ask beyond our greatest prayers or verbalize them. He requires us to expand our expectations. We should not see the purpose, judge and give all manner of reasons, or looking back on the crying and wailing years.

You will find life-giving purpose and meaning when you allow God to take your painful experiences and comfort others. You will be able to share a unique hope because you know exactly what it feels like to be them.

God's counsel shall stand. God can carry out what he says he will do. Simply believe.

A lady called me and requested me to pray for her. "My son has unusual cancer, intimal sarcoma. He has gone through surgery and chemo, and has started radiation as a final medication for his treatment. The doctors have given him less than six months or less. Please pray that he will be cured of this awful disease!"

The whys when nothing makes sense lead us to our wits' end, but it's not without purpose. Your brain takes you on a road trip and fills you with doubt, but thank God for his Spirit that quickens to fix your eyes on the only anchor and hope.

Free Will

God is not the author of evil and doesn't want you or me to parent in sorrow. His blessings add no sorrow: "Children are a gift from the Lord; they are a reward from him" (Psalm 127:3). As we deepen our understanding of faith, it is paramount to understand that God has given us free will, and our children have it too. What better assurance for a parent in pain than in the promises of God's Word. Yes, have faith in God, but there is a warning on lack of understanding or the exegesis of scripture, which Merriam-Webster's Dictionary explains as the critical explanation or interpretation of a text especially of scripture.

For many years I struggled with understanding faith in the context of my parenting journey. The more I tried to memorize it, the more it did not make sense—until I proposed to take God at his word and believe his promises concerning my children and me. "The seed of the righteous is blessed."(Psalm 37:26b). In this psalm, to some extent, David knew and understood hardship. This promise is comforting to you and me as parents! David further expounds from his life as a young boy tending the sheep. He killed a lion and a bear, and his amazing testimony is worth emulating for parents. Psalm 37:25 says, "I have been young, and now am old, yet I have not seen the righteous forsaken or his children begging for bread."

Two dimensions of faith or faithfulness are developed in Hebrews 11 through the Hebrew heroes, who remarkably exhibited faith: "Now faith is the assurance of things hoped for, the conviction of things not seen" (Hebrews 11:1).

Faith provides a guarantee, the peg on which we hang our hopes. Our hope is not a flimsy dream, but through faith it is real and has substance. Through it, we have ground to hold fast in our parenting journey, launching to the deep. It propels us to the unknown, keeping our hope alive.

Faith Moves Us Forward

The stories of Abel, Enoch, Noah, Abraham, and Sarah show us that faithfulness requires both holding fast and moving forward. First, faithfulness is holding fast to the promises of God. God had promised Sarah and Abraham countless descendants and land that God would reveal to them. But both stakes were "things not seen" (Hebrews 11:1).

Are you contemplating and thinking that the situation for your child is out of hand? Would God give these wanderers from your descendants as numerous as stars in the sky and as countless as the grains of sand on the seashore (Hebrews 11:12)?

Perhaps Abraham could still father a child, but Sarah knew her childbearing days were many, many years in the past. That is why she laughed so hard the first time she overheard their visitors tell Abraham he would soon be a father. That is why their son's name would be Isaac, which meant "laughter." His name marked God's joy in upending human expectations. Abraham and Sarah also held fast to a second promise, that of land. That promise was equally impossible, for these two were wanderers, pilgrims who set out not knowing their destination. Even when they arrived in the promised land of Canaan, they lived like strangers in a foreign country, in tents, always ready to pack up and move.

But they did more than hold fast to this promise. Sarah and Abraham knew that the promise of God is also a call, so they lived out the second dimension of faithfulness, that of moving forward. They lived in tents because they were not ultimately called to the land of Canaan. That was not their final destination. The journey was part of their obedience, but Canaan was not their home. They were looking for another city, the city with foundations not made with hands, "whose architect and builder is God" (Hebrews 11:10).

They did not receive that promise in their lifetime. They saw only the commitment on the horizon, beckoning, calling them onward in their journey. Because they experienced the promise as a call, they held fast to the promises of God, and they also moved forward in response to God's call. They knew that faithfulness is a form of courage that launches out into the unknown, moving into the future with God, knowing the future of your child is in the hands of God.

This act of faith is an excellent example of holding on to God's promises. Can we measure up to these dimensions of faith? Some of us may find it easy to respond to the promises, but it is hard for others to hold fast. Still, our dependence is from God. We may not be fond of tents, and we cannot afford to travel with lots of baggage.

There is a victory when we walk with God. "Be strong and courageous. God commands us to be strong and courageous" (Joshua 1:8–9).

A parent in pain may have little trouble moving forward. There is a temptation to camp and to travel light. We ask,

"Where can we join what God is doing now?" We are a people on the way, on the move, knowing that the future belongs to God, but we need help holding fast, learning the story of God's faithfulness to promise. We need to know of loyalty and endurance and persevere even when the journey is dark and long, and the lights are dim.

You and I need both dimensions of faithfulness. You and I need to hold fast to the promises of God. Believe in moving forward into the future, which is God's. The power of the example of Sarah and Abraham is that their lives were anchored in. Amid change and uncertainty, they found God constant and faithful. Sometimes all you and I need is to act. That action we have to take can flip the switch! The journey may be longer than anticipated, and we may not be out of the woods yet where Satan still has his moments.

By unwavering faith, the world is conquered, the fiery darts of the enemy are quenched, souls are saved, and lives are changed. By faith as we journey through life, when we set the Lord always before us, the invisible God becomes real and present in our minds and lives. This shift and transformation removes the mountains ahead because at the presence of the Lord, at the presence of the God of Jacob, the mountains were not only moved but removed: "The mountains skipped like rams, the hills like lambs. What ails you, O sea, that you flee? O Jordan, that you turn back? O mountains, that you skip like rams? O hills, like lambs? Tremble, O earth, at the presence of the Lord, at the presence of the God of Jacob, who turns the rock into a pool of water, the flint into a spring of water" (Psalm 114:4–7).

Jesus's Assurance

God speaks through his Word. In the seasons of parenting when nothing makes sense, the devil can cloud our minds with discouraging thoughts, building pictures of failure, fear, and no hope or purpose for a wayward child. The same happened to the disciples of Jesus when they came upon a man who had been born blind. "Who sinned?" they asked Jesus. "This man or his parents?" (John 9:1–2). The disciples wanted a reason for the man's blindness because they assumed sin must have caused it. If you are like me, you want answers for most situations to justify why something happens. Like the disciples wanted the significance of the man's blindness, you want to know why your child's current position is what it is.

Jesus assured His disciples the man's blindness, just like in Job's case, was part of the glorious works of God, which would be revealed. Jesus fulfilled his claim by spiritually and physically healing him. "'Neither this man nor his parents sinned,' said Jesus, 'but this happened so that the works of God might be displayed in him ... While I am in the world, I am the light of the world'" (John 9:3–5).

The emotional pain felt from a child's distraction may feel like a "thorn in the flesh," as Apostle Paul states, but this pruning takes our self-reliance and self-absorption to an opportunity for opening your spiritual eyes to see through the eyes of faith the glory of God, as assured by Jesus and Job. "Consider it pure joy, my brothers and sisters, whenever you face trials of many kinds because you know that the testing of your faith produces perseverance. Let perseverance finish its work so that you may be mature and complete, not lacking anything" (James 1:2–4).

Countless times you and I desire trouble-free parenting journeys and, above all, joy. Nevertheless, joy is a by-product reaped by having faith in God and the truth of his Word. Today in the world, there are songs of happiness, maybe well-intended, but they end up as deadly recipes of bad theology, drawing our hearts further away from God. In these days of social media, we do our best. We take pictures, edit, crop, edit again, and post the perfect shot. We see the charade. We make-believe it can be a perfect family, child, or moment that puts a smile in us from God.

We do not live in a perfect world, as Jesus taught to his disciples: "I have said these things to you, so that in me you may have peace. In this world, you will have tribulation. But take heart! I have overcome the world" (John 16:33). By this saying, the disciples amazingly improved in faith and knowledge. They knew not their own weakness, just as we may assume our Christian walk as believers guarantees only happiness. To keep it real and honest in this world, we encounter job loss, parenting challenges, sickness, wayward children, and many more challenges.

The theological interpretation may not make sense to a wailing mother, a grieving parent, a patient in the ICU, and many issues causing mental and emotional anguish. "Be of good cheer" gives comfort to the heart. The divine nature of God has not deserted the human nature but supports and comforts it!

Matthew Henry, in his biblical commentary, states that God's reassures us of his presence when we feel forsaken by the world. Peace in Christ is the only true peace; in him alone, we believers of Christ have peace with God, and so in him we have peace in our own minds. This is encouraging because Christ has overcome the world before us.

Challenging and stormy moments don't make weak faith; they make us even more aware of our need to press into faith in God. He is our perfect peace!

Peace with God through Faith

> Therefore, since we have been justified by faith, we have peace with God through our Lord Jesus Christ. Through him, we have also obtained access by faith into this grace in which we stand, and we rejoice in the hope of the glory of God.
>
> Not only that, but we rejoice in our sufferings, knowing that suffering produces endurance, and

endurance produces character, and character produces hope,

and hope does not put us to shame because God's love has been poured into our hearts through the Holy Spirit who has been given to us. (Romans 5:1–5)

Jealous God

"So they feared LORD, but they also served their own gods in after the matter of the nations from among whom they have had been carried away" (2 Kings 17:33).

Today's sad reality is that many of us are worshipping God but are still stuck in some traditional parenting strongholds. We go to church, yet still we believe in traditional healers, horoscopes, palm readings, tea leaf readings, witch doctors, spell casters, and ancestors. In ignorance, we insist on mixing darkness with light. This cannot be! Parents teach and train children in Godly ways to learn a new perspective regarding what it means to grow through tough seasons.

With God, you have to believe in his sovereignty and in his supremacy. You can't have a plan B just in case it doesn't work out with God and the situation seems senseless. You can't still be bowing down to idols yet say you're a Christian, because we know that he's a jealous God. He clearly tells us in his Word that we shall not bow before any other God.

Some of it looks like harmless family traditions, yet they can be doctrines of devils. It looks like just culture, yet it's bondage. We need to be Christians who refuse to compromise. We can't believe in superstitions and believe in the Bible at the same time. Some of us are kept in bondage by these questionable family traditions. We wonder why there's no fruit on our Christian walk. Well, there you have it! If you're still visiting shrines and occultists and bowing down to and worshiping dead people, you are in idolatry. Break away from these dangerous traditions. Be set free! There's no fellowship between light and darkness. There's nothing that those demons, which are masquerading as power, can offer you. It's only bondage! Refuse to do those incarnations and ceremonies that you don't understand. Be the light in your family.

Faith Is a Language That God Understands

Beloved, faith is when you give the testimony before seeing a physical manifestation of what God promised you. Faith is when you start prophesying unto your situation and declaring God's Word upon it. Faith is when you are in the middle of a storm, but you are telling the storm to cease because you know he's given you the power to do so. Faith is a language that God understands. Meanwhile, fear is the language that the devil understands. Which language do you speak?

I dare you to start speaking the things that are not as though they are. I dare you to start testifying about your current parental journey. "But the more I pray, the more the situation gets worse!" Friend, declare God's promises upon your child and wait upon the manifestation of his Word. Numbers 23:19 states, "God is not a man that he should lie or a son of man that he should change his mind."

Though you haven't seen any change or even gotten feedback on their whereabouts, I dare you to start speaking to that sickness, telling it who your God is. With no doubt, believe that his stripes heal you. I dare you to say unto your family and marriage that went sour due to children's detours that the blame game is not helping the situation. Speak the Word and tell the devil that what therefore God has joined together, let not separate (Mark 10:9). I dare you to speak to your womb. Tell it to hear the Word of the Lord when he commanded that we be fruitful and multiply. Don't go with what you can see in your child's situation, because the things that we can see are temporary, but the things we can't see are eternal (1 Corinthians 4:18). Take up your shield of faith because without it, you are vulnerable to the fiery darts of the enemy, and without it, it's impossible to please the Lord.

It is easier to trust God in the good times. It takes much more faith to keep that trust during painful trials. Tough times happen to everyone. It is sometimes difficult to believe that God is willing to take you through the impossible situations in your life. But faith is the most essential thing that you must have in this age of crisis and turmoil. The peace of God that transcends all understanding is predicated on believing that God's Word is right.

Without faith, it is impossible to please God because trust is the key to all the strength and power God has to give us. It merely means that you believe that God is bigger than your problems.

Today, start meditating on his Word and ask him to illuminate your heart with his truth. Trust that he is good and has good things in store for your future, because faith is what pleases God. Study the Bible, and by doing so, your faith will grow, and you will start pleasing him by resting in power but not in the wisdom of humans. "So that your faith might not rest in the wisdom of men but in the power of God" (1 Corinthians 2:5).

Parents, your faith counts. Keep praying, sharpen your faith, and listen to God's Word, and your faith will be nothing short of credible. Faith is a game changer in our parenting journey, as one of my heroes and generals of faith, Dr. Tony Evans, in his preaching online at Oak Cliff Bible Fellowship in Dallas, Texas, once stated, "Trusting God when things don't make sense is a decision. Faith is a decision."

8

We Do Not Know What to Do, but Our Eyes Are on You

> Nothing fruitful ever comes when plants are forced to flower in the wrong season.
> —Bette Bao Lord

In despair as a parent, what do you do? The odds were not suitable for Jehoshaphat, and honestly, they are not that great for many parents right now.

King Jehoshaphat, an Old Testament king, received word that three armies had conspired together and were coming against him in one massive assault. He made a decisive and unconventional leadership move.

> And Jehoshaphat stood in the assembly of Judah and Jerusalem, in the house of the Lord, before the new court, and said, "O Lord, God of our fathers, are you not God in Heaven? You rule over the kingdoms of the nations. In your hands are power and might, so that no one can to withstand you ... we will stand before this house -and cry out

> to you in affliction, and you will hear and save,
> O our God. Will you do not execute judgment on
> them? For we are powerless against this great
> horde that is coming against us. We do not know
> what to do, but our eyes are on you." (2 Chronicles
> 20:5–12)

Deep down, most parents who have weathered the storms of parenting know that we will get through, but it is not a walk in the park. We will endure the carnage and detours and emerge from the depths to grow and keep journeying again. Does the journey ever stop? No, but it takes longer than expected sometimes—a long time. Right now, you may feel like you are in the valley of the shadow of death. However, you are not alone.

So how do you parent through these dark hours? Let us examine what Jehoshaphat chose to do first in his dark hour. First and foremost, he called the people to seek God. The king prayed this transformational, twelve-word prayer: "We do not know what to do, but our eyes are on you" (2 Chronicles 20:12).

Focusing on what the Bible says about parenting when you are in the midst of a downward spiral with your child can be difficult. Nevertheless, by staying engaged with the Lord and praying amid the detours, your struggle is key to being the parent your child needs you to be, and it sets an excellent example for your child.

By now, there are too many questions about critical the parenting issues we have discussed. Let us see what our Master said: "Then Jesus came to them and said, 'All authority in Heaven and on earth has been given to me. Therefore go and make disciples of all nations, baptizing them in the name of the Father and of the Son and the Holy Spirit, and teaching them to obey everything I have commanded you. Moreover, surely I am with you always, to the very end of the age'" (Matthew 28:18–20)

These transformational words from Jesus are for leading in unprecedented parenting times. Jesus assures you of his presence and rest! Can there be rest in the middle of the storm? Yes, he rests himself and promises peace in our hard realities, as discussed earlier. It is unnecessary to retreat to the desert or a mountaintop, either temporarily or permanently, to find spiritual refreshment. Jesus said if we would but come to him for living water or rest (Matthew 11:28–30), we would find it in abundance. We can create that place of rest in an area of prayer, Bible study, meditation, or worship—anywhere we can retreat from the cares and busyness of life. When we turn over those cares to God in prayer through Christ, "do not be anxious about anything; but in everything but by prayer and supplication with thanksgiving, let your requests be made known unto God" (Philippians 4:6). "And the peace of God, which surpass all understanding will guard your heart and your minds in Christ Jesus" (Philippians 4:7).

Parents, obedience is serious business with God: "Continue steadfastly in prayer, being watchful in it with thanksgiving" (Colossians 4:2). Taking the time to fellowship with God in prayer brings rest.

Satan wants you stressed, worn out, and compromised by feeling angry and overloaded. A friend asked me a while back about my loud absence on one of the social media platforms. I did not mince my words and knew what to say: it was intentional. Such a comment could go in many ways. I was not sure whether that question was out of concern, but what was considered absent was a choice of being productive.

The intention was not to be defensive or prideful, but it was the truth. I looked back at the technology days, and no doubt the "no tech days" paid off. Yes, I chose to master health promotion and study abroad without the limelight of a selfie post on social media. "Mom, you are at the Eiffel Tower," my son noted.

As I write this, a perfect message was preached on my favorite morning radio program by Dr. Evans at Oak Cliff Bible Fellowship in Dallas, Texas. It came from his daily radio morning ministry, *The Urban Alternative*. "The freedom to choose is not the freedom to determine the outcome of those choices. Oftentimes when we find ourselves searching for a U-turn or hoping a reversal or calling for God to deliver us, we forget that it was our own choices that got us lost to begin with. And when we forget that, we also forget to come before the Lord in a spirit of humility rather than entitlement."

Is this not true of you and me and our children? We have choices while we are waiting: we can choose not to wait alone, choose our mood and outlook, choose to trust, choose our thoughts, or choose our behavior. Have you listened to a preacher and thought, "This message is for me"? Determining whatever was lovely and shifting my focus from the detour to a powerful and gracious God was the key. After that, I wrote a thesis paper and completed my master's education in health promotion. I had a lot to accomplish with my studies without all the limelight and pretending that all was well outside; I was bleeding on the inside.

It is possible to make a choice when desperate or in need, to accomplish something for the short or long haul. Though the storms may rage and life seems like swimming against the tide, it is possible to be intentional and make a choice to have a divine encounter each morning. We can have "no tech" days but cannot afford a "no spiritual" moment. How do you jump-start your day? Do you start it by being God conscious, or do you browse the stock market?

In my storm, I have "no tech" Tuesdays and Thursdays. I chose to read God's Word and enrolled in biblical counselling classes. In those classes, I deafened the stormy parenting moments by an in-depth study of God's Word. In the course of the eighteen-month study, I made meaningful relationships with raw, honest conversations about my parental struggles. I cut out lots of time with curious people or conversations that were spiced with judgment and masked with "I am praying for you."

While driving on Route 66, I was amazed by God's desire for my location and my desires. In his presence, I basked in unconditional love, not in others' words, judgment, and opinions.

"I cried aloud to the Lord and he answered me from his holy hill. Selah" (Psalm 3:4).

Some may call it theology, but biblical wisdom and real prayer time were birthed in those eighteen months. It is a spiritual investment not worth trading for anything rosy looking that the world offers. This was not just reading the entire Bible in six months. It was using the uncompromised Word of God as my fighting tools to parent. Did it change my child's situation? Maybe not, but I changed my parental perspective. There was spiritual growth and development, and better still raw growth and maturity. I was no longer tossed or discouraged. The race continues with endurance fighting on my knees, and with other sisters easing the journey. "Iron sharpens iron, and one man sharpens another" (Proverbs 27:17).

The fall's beginning is a breath of fresh air. The season wakes us to wonderful, chilly, refreshing mornings full of promise. Would it be awesome if our parenting days and journeys felt the same?

It is humanly possible. If you start your day with God's Word, spending time with him, you can walk out the door refreshed and with enough energy to start your day right. Take the time to seek him before you start your day. His promises hold a lot more than just a chilly morning. "Be not wise in your own eyes; fear the Lord and turn away from evil. It will be healing to your flesh and refreshment to your bones" (Proverbs 3:7–8).

The Promises of God

I would be lying if I said this is how to parent from my experience, but pointing you to God's truth has never failed, and it always makes sense with a spiritual perspective. What do you learn in your journey? You can never go wrong leaning on God's promises; his representations are sure and firm. They are unchanging, unwavering, and unmovable. For the sake of his name, he does fulfill his promises, because he is faithful and true. Therefore we can say yes and amen. "For all the promises of God find their Yes in him. That is why it is through him that we utter our Amen to God for his glory" (2 Corinthians 1:20).

I reference a list by one of my favorite authors, Lysa Terkeurst in her book *It's Not Supposed to Be* (p. 188), regarding the areas where the enemy tries to gain a foothold over us, but we fight back with the words.

> Affection—my heart, what I love
> Adoration—my mouth, what I worship
> Attention—my mind, what I focus on
> Attraction—my eyes, what I desire
> Ambition—my calling, what I spend my time seeking
> Action—my choices, how I stand firm

Truth is vital to our victory in our journey and our children's lives. The psalmist assures us, "The LORD is near to all who call on him, to all who call on him in truth" (Psalm 145:18).

Prayer of Surrender

The truth of God's Word and your prayers may not change what you see in your naked eyes, but they change how you see. This revelation transformed the way I took my parenting role—with total surrender!

> Dear God, I lift my tearful eyes to you. Please disrupt my false sense of control and my overblown confidence in my abilities. I humbly bow and ask for your supernatural strength, wisdom, and courage so I can endure these hard days and lead myself, my children, and my family with faith for the future. My daily prayer is that I don't know what to do, but my eyes are on you.

> Lead me and use me as an agent for your glory. In Jesus's name, amen.

> I cannot do this. It is too much, Lord. I give up trying to fix it!

> Take my child. Mold my child into your image and let my child conform to your will. May your plan and purpose prevail. You are the potter, and my child is clay.

When you have reached your breaking point as I did, you realize that things are out of your control. That is when God will show you that he is in total control.

Sing if you have to, like the hymn written by Eddie Espinosa.

> Change My Heart All, Lord!
> Make it ever true
> Change my heart, oh God.
> May I be like You
> You are the potter
> I am the clay
> Mold me and make me
> This is what I pray

As a parent, allow God to change the heart of your child. In our parenting journey, we will get disappointed and hurt, and we will face many trials. But we will always have God support us, help us, and lead us to overcome. What seems impossible for man is never impossible for God. It is possible to have full joy amid hard realities, as stated by Apostle John:

> That which was from the beginning, which we have heard, which we have seen with our eyes, which we have looked upon, and our hands have handled, of the Word of life; For the life was manifested, and we have seen it, and bear witness,

> and show unto you that eternal life, which was
> with the Father and was manifested unto us;)
> That which we have seen and heard declare we
> unto you, that ye also may have fellowship with
> us: and truly our fellowship is with the Father,
> and with his Son Jesus Christ. And these things
> write we unto you that your joy may be full. (1
> John 1:1–4)

So do it right and journey on with courage, but face it head-on. Weep if you have to, but get back up! Laugh, watch, pray, love, live, give thanks and praise, mend, and honor. Remember that God's Word is true and is essential, and you cannot live without it. It is like oxygen.

Prayer Requests

"Naomi visited Leny's grave with her daughter Chichi and one of the grandchildren. Please continue to keep Michael's family in your prayers; their son struggles with substance abuse."

The prayer requests are endless and come from text messages.

> Please lift my son Duke in your prayers. My son
> Duke was diagnosed with COVID-19; he has
> pneumonia and is currently on a ventilator. My
> family has not been able to see him at the hospital.
> The only word they give us—he is now in a coma
> and will not survive. I feel a death sentence has
> been passed! It does not make sense!

There is nothing as painful as a hopeless situation in humans' eyes, but God does not want to see us stuck in our pain. Although it is more complicated, it is also more important than ever to be hopeful during the struggle. God wants to bring us through, not see us get stuck in pain.

Christian clichés—Platitudes and False Comfort

Who has the tidy answers to a hurting mother or explanations of why a friend's daughter committed suicide? The daughter is nowhere to be found and homeless. Sarah Waters states, "And perhaps there is a limit to the grieving that the human heart can do. As when one adds salt to a tumbler of water, there comes a point where simply no more will be absorbed" (Sarah Waters, *The Little Strangers*, 2009).

Some throw out Christian clichés and platitudes. God loves good things too, and some words are best not said to a hurting parent painting a furious, mean God. The ministry of silence, a hug, or a handshake is a better alternative. How can a loving Father break into pieces the heart of loving parents?

"All things work together for good" (Romans 8:28). All things, whether joy or pain, poverty or riches, and the million changes of life, are truly together for spiritual and eternal good. We live in a fallen world, and trials, pain, and suffering are part of our package. When we are faced with a crisis in parenting, what does God do? Jehoshaphat and Moses knew very well that question can be answered with one word: fight. But fight from victory! "His job is to fight. Our job is to trust. God fights for us and our children and families. He assures us and says, 'Remain calm, the Lord will fight for you'" (Exodus 14:14). Continue to trust our Lord and Savior and his tremendous power to save your son, restore your daughter to health, and strengthen your children.

The Latter Glory

Our latter days cannot help but be more significant than our former days, not because of anything in us but because the glory of God rains upon and touches every part of our lives. For our God is a God of finishing. The Lord shall restore. Joel 2:25–27 says,

> I will repay you for the years the locusts have eaten
> the great locust and the young locust,
> the other locusts and the locust swarm
> the great army that I sent among you.
> You will have plenty to eat until you are full,
> and you will praise the name of the Lord your God,
> who has worked wonders for you;
> never again will my people be shamed.
> Then you will know that I am in Israel,
> that I am the Lord (I) your God,
> and that there is no other;
> never again will my people be shamed.

All-Knowing God

You know those unknowns in your life that keep stealing both your peace and your sleep? You don't have to keep trying to figure those things out, my friend. Something that encourages me deeply is remembering that God knows all things in their entirety. There is nothing hidden from God. And because God knows all things and sees all things, only he sees the big picture; we see in part. Over the last few years, God has encouraged me not to lose heart in my parenting journey. He is continually bringing me to rest in him, and as Paul stated, when we endure and persevere in our ambassadorial calling, we have a reward awaiting us. "For our light and momentary troubles are achieving for us an eternal glory that far outweighs them all" (2 Corinthians 4:17). I have learned from this parenting season that it does not matter your parenting outcome when nothing makes sense. No matter how hard parenting gets, God will get the ultimate glory, and all the waiting hardships and troubles will be worth it.

9

Pray For Me, I am A Parent

Trading our will for "thy will" because we know He will.

—Lysa Terkeurst

I want to admit something to you that I'm not proud of. Unlike both my late grandmothers, who were low-key and a great testament of Godly contentment, sometimes I struggle to trust God with my children. Yes, I do! There's something so hard about this for me. Though I have complete faith in God, when it comes down to the nitty-gritty of fully trusting his plans with my children, I fall short. I worry. I get incredibly anxious. I make lots of suggestions to God on their behalf. I try to keep things in their world calm free of hurt and on track toward some "best plan" I've imagined for them. It's like I gather up my people in my arms and tell God, "See? I've got it all worked out. Now, if you'll bless all this—don't mess with it, just bless it—then my children's lives will be good."

I'm slowly learning how to grab hold of the only plan that is foolproof with my children, even now that they are adults (and one teenager): to truly entrust them to the Lord.

The very best thing a parent can do is recognize only God

is good at being God. And the best way to protect our children is to show them what it looks like to trust God in the good, bad, and ugly circumstances—and better still, when the storms of life come raging at us. A common phrase says there are three categories of people: "You are just coming out of a storm," "You are going through a storm" and "You are about to get into a storm." These are the hard realities of life, are they not?

As I write this book, the first and second categories describe my life situation. I was spared from the jaws of death via the deadly COVID-19 virus by God's healing mercies. He gave me a second chance and is the reason for this book. The second reality is that the effects of the global pandemic are real! I am not sure of your category, but as my home church pastor, David Welch, preached, "Life is hard because it is an endurance race, and hitting the wall is a real experience." Discouragement is real, it will come to your life, but you do not have to give in to it. With the weapon of prayer, God's promises, and Jesus in you, you will overcome."

Burden Bearers

But there is hope! There is help! Look around. There is a burden bearer the Lord has positioned to bear your burden and feed your spirit. The burden bearer may seem to have no financial resources, but that person is well able to lift you in prayer and give you a shoulder to cry on, as simple and deep as saying "pray for me, I am a parent". Help is not equated only to monetary value in matters of the heart. Why are there more suicide deaths among the affluent in society? The spotlight on celebrities and depression is statistically evident. Could it be an issue of identity crisis and ruminations of self-worth? Truth be told, many people define themselves by their pursuits, from their jobs to their relationships.

Apostle Paul was always praying for the believers he met on his missions. He viewed intercession as a privilege. You and

I need someone to pray for us even as we take time to have personal devotion. Colossians 1:9–10 states, "For this reason, we also, since the day we heard it, do not cease to pray for you, and to ask that you may be filled with the knowledge of His will in all wisdom and spiritual understanding; that you may walk worthy of the Lord, fully pleasing Him, being fruitful in every good work and increasing in the knowledge of God."

They were praying in the name of the Lord with expectations for the miraculous. "After they prayed, the place where they were meeting was shaken. And they were all filled with the Holy Spirit and spoke the Word of God boldly" (Acts 4:31).

Humility and Vulnerability

Humility does not equate to weakness. Instead, it is where we find our strength. Better yet, humility is the place we access God's supply. When your car has a flat tire at 1:00 a.m., whom will you call? God is a source of strength to go to. It doesn't hurt to say every once in a while to our spouses, prayer partners, and trusted friends, "I am not okay. I need help and prayers. I am hurting." It is an icebreaker to the next cause of action because some problems may need more intervention than just prayer. Will you simply pray for a suicidal person? Absolutely not. Call for emergency help first!

This posture of humility is essential because it positions us for supernatural assistance. "A word came to the king, and a battle plan was set in motion. Jehoshaphat was told, 'You will not have to fight this battle. Take up your positions, stand firm, and see the deliverance the Lord will give you. Do not be afraid; do not be discouraged. Go out to face them tomorrow, and the Lord will be with you'" (2 Chronicles 20:17). Check out all the active verbs. Take up your position. Stand firm. Look. Go out. Face them.

Associate with people with positive energy—your burden bearers! Minimize the time you spend with negative people.

Emotions are contagious. Help others, but don't carry anybody's emotional baggage. You have your own bucket of issues to deal with.

To say you could walk alone in the lonely journey would be jumping from the pan and into the fire. Two to three trusted friends to speak of God's unfailing truth through the spoken Word lifts the burden. It takes vulnerability and trust. Trusted sisters, brothers, or faith family to pray for you and me!

The Spirit Sustains

The psalmist explicitly explains that "the spirit will sustain his infirmity; but a wounded spirit who can bear?" (Psalm 18:14)

Your spirit is a two-edged sword. It can cut away life's troubles and leave you happy and on top of the world. Alternatively, it can slice your soul to where the pain is indescribable. It is your wisdom to keep your spirit with all diligence so that you can use it for your profit.

When Job ruled his spirit, he worshipped and blessed God, though his circumstances were terrible (Job 1:20–22). When Job let his spirit run wild with thoughts about his significant losses, he cursed the day he was born and wished he were dead (Job 3:1–26). And he went downhill from there until Elihu and God corrected his self-justification and self-pity (Job 32:2; 38:1–3). His Spirit first sustained him, and then it nearly destroyed him. A wounded spirit is more painful than a wounded body, for the soul is more vital to your happiness. If the spirit is wounded and hurting, it does not matter how healthy and firm your body might be. If you allow any difficulty or sorrow to gain victory over your spirit, the crushing pain can be intolerable. Fools will seek the comfort of bodily death.

Ruled and directed by wisdom, your spirit can help you survive any difficulty. Allowed to judge you when wounded, it is unbearable to you and others. Ruled and directed by the Spirit of God, you can be cheerful in any adversity. Allowed to run free, it can and will drive even conscientious men toward suicide. Are you ruling your spirit today?

Natural humans have done incredible things under horrible stress, pain, danger, and difficulty because of their strong and courageous spirits. Their exploits are lovely to read, but a Christian can do better. The knowledge of present reality and future expectations and the Spirit of Christ's sustaining help are things the wicked know nothing about.

Ruling your spirit is the best evidence of Christian maturity and the means to help others. Fighting heretics or troubles on the outside is easy. Overseeing an angry, impulsive, melancholy, or offended spirit on the inside is much more difficult. Growing in grace and walking in the Holy Spirit to bear his fruit will result in the wise rule of your spirit.

Nothing you do in life is as important as ruling your spirit. If you let it rule, you are a loser (Proverbs 25:28). If you judge it, you are more significant than a man who defeats a city himself (Proverbs 16:32). Your spirit is the vital force behind your benefit to others or your burden to them. Your spirit can arm you to accomplish great things or keep you from ever being useful.

His Word Illuminates

Truly God is the author of our lives and our children's lives. His Word is the only prescription powerful enough to empower us. Parents, it is not about you and me! It is not about your feelings, wants, and needs. It is not about your happiness, satisfaction, and contentment in your parenting journey. It cannot be about our dreams and successes, our success in avoiding suffering, or our achievements in our families.

But is it wrong to desire personal success, peace, health, the right family, and healthy relationships? Good question! There is nothing wrong in these things so long as Christ takes preeminence. When we allow them to rule our hearts and journeys, they take center stage of our hearts, and we sadly replace God. We offer microwave prayers, expecting instant prayers for our self-oriented visions for ourselves and family.

Letting go and easing up on control is not always the easy road taken, but our best job as parents is to be obedient to God. God's job is everything else because his will is well stated by Apostle Paul: "For from him and through him and to him are all things. To him be glory forever. Amen" (Romans 11:36). As you and I pray for our children, ourselves, and our families, let us usher in and celebrate the Lord and not ourselves.

Some verses are hard, but his Word illuminates your heart,is holistic, as stated in 2 Timothy 3:16–17, "All scripture is breathed out by God and profitable for teaching, for reproof, for correction and training in righteousness, that the man of God may be complete, equipped for every good work."

The Application of Prayer

Prayer is our most intimate time with the person who loves us the most. I look back over my life and can't believe how many years passed that I didn't pray to God daily. Mistakes were made, and paths that I traveled were not of God's doing because I relied on my limited knowledge and what I thought was best. I strongly encourage all my friends and family to seek the good Lord daily.

Prayer is our direct line of communication with Father God. In worship, we can praise, thank, and ask God to direct our steps. There are times in our lives when bad things happen; death, divorce, loss of a job, betrayal, and sickness hit us or our loved ones. In prayer, we ask God, "Why?" We vent, cry out for help, and seek guidance. Regardless of whether we are rejoicing in the good Lord or can barely say a word from being so lost, when the pain is so great, God is still there listening, waiting to console us. Apostle Paul said, "Pray without ceasing" (1 Thessalonians 5:17). If we want to know God and have a personal relationship with him and his Son, Jesus, we have to pray consistently and routinely read our Bibles. In prayer, we get our marching orders from God regarding how to proceed with life, whether it's a big decision or a smaller decision.

The one thing about prayer is we may feel lonely, forgotten about, lost, or unimportant, but God hears us when no one else does. He genuinely cares about us and wants to give us the desires of our hearts in a way that enriches us and glorifies him. A prayer is a powerful tool with God. God is the Great Healer, the Great Provider, the Great Supporter, and the best friend we can ever have. God loves us all unconditionally and truly wants the best for our lives.

Biblical Pattern of Prayer

The Lord's Prayer is a guide to pray according to God's will.

> Our Father in heaven,
> hallowed be your name.
> Your kingdom come,
> your will be done,
> on earth as it is in heaven.
> Give us this day our daily bread,
> and forgive us our debts,
> as we also have forgiven our debtors.
> And lead us not into temptation,
> but deliver us from evil.

It warms my heart to watch my sons' conversations with their daddy from the latest basketball playoffs to the current football season. Sometimes there are heated arguments with bets on anticipated wins. The boys, as we fondly called them, are now young men and have no reservations voicing their needs, whether it be their tight budget, their college education, current dating lives, fears, or aspirations. My calm, collected husband has a listening ear and gives advice and sometimes tough love. The free communication and assurance that their daddy is always available and creates time for them in a loving manner is the glue that draws grown young men to their daddy. Have there been disappoints and limitations along the parenting process? Absolutely! Having two college children was not a butter and bread season! "But God!" That was a breath of fresh air.

Now, if an earthly father can be so approachable and loving, how about our heavenly Father who is immutable, never changes, is infinite and omnipotent, is everywhere, is unlimited, and is all-powerful, and above is personal? We pray, and know that he listens!

Pray Like Jesus Taught

The Lord's Prayer is a prayer to God, our Father. Jesus taught his disciples the Lord's Prayer as an example of how you pray, and he gave "ingredients" that should go into prayer. "Our father in heaven" is teaching us whom to address our prayers to: the Father. "Hallowed be your name" is telling us to worship God and praise him for who he is. "Your Kingdom come, your will be done on earth as it is in heaven" is a reminder to us that we are to pray for God's plan in our lives and the world, not our own plan. We are to pray for God's will to be done, not our desires. How many times have you and I prayed out of our own desires? With these guidelines, you have a better understanding on prayer.

Teach your child to pray like Jesus taught. Pray simply but deeply to a loving Father, God. He will do more than we dare ask or think, going beyond our greatest dreams, hopes, and prayers! You have the power, and God will answer your prayers and exceed them, as Apostle Paul states in Ephesians 3:20–21, "Now to him who is able to do far more abundantly than all that we ask or think, according to the power at work within us, to him be glory in the church and in Christ Jesus throughout all generations, forever and ever. Amen."

Saving Grace

First, we have to submit ourselves to him and accept his Son, Jesus Christ, as our Lord and Savior. Then we have the gift of forgiveness, eternal life, and direct communication with him through prayer. If you have never accepted Jesus as your Lord and Savior, unfortunately you do not have those three blessings. You can pray, but God may or may not bless you in your prayer. His response is going to be one of salvation, meaning he will convict your heart that you are lost and separated from the Father and Son because of not accepting Jesus as your Lord and Savior. Don't waste another day not getting God's best or being separated from God. Pray the sinner's prayer and ask Jesus to come into your life and be your Lord!

It is not an understatement when I say I do not know how to be a wife, a mother, a career woman, or a friend without Jesus. As stated in Psalm 46:1, "God is our refuge and strength, a very present help in trouble." Also, Jesus Christ said, "You are my friends if you do what I command you" (John 15:14)

You can be born again in Christ and have the blessings of eternal life, forgiveness, direct communication with God, and so much more! In closing, Jesus said this about the importance of prayer: "Ask, and it will be given to you; seek, and you will find; knock, and it will be opened to you" (Matthew 7:7–8).

Do not be casual about your prayer life. You can take anything and everything to God in prayer through Jesus Christ. Take all of your parenting journey to the Lord in prayer. You can give thanksgiving for who he is, ask for forgiveness, fight fear and doubts, focus on his promises, and pray according to his Word to feed your faith in the journey. As written by Apostle Paul, "So faith comes from hearing, and hearing through the word of Christ" (Romans 10:17). Along the same lines, God's faithfulness is demonstrated in David's prayer in the book of Samuel: "Because of your promise, and according to your own heart, you have brought about all this greatness, to make your servant know it. Therefore you are great, O Lord God. For there is none like you, and there is no God besides you, according to all that we have heard with our ears" (2 Samuel 7:21–22).

Often when we pray, God shows himself in unimaginable ways and exceeds our human expectations. He is greater than previously revealed and magnifies his Word above his name. This is well stated in Psalm 138:2, "I bow down toward your holy temple and give thanks to your name for your steadfast love and your faithfulness, for you have exalted above all things your name and your word."

Discover the Power of Prayer

Why pray? In a society that is full of many voices and choices, many have run to idols for solutions and abandoned faith in God.

Being a parent and an agent of great things in your children's lives can create a spiritual culture and legacy of prayer in the good, bad, and ugly moments. A constant communication to God is essential for the spiritual growth and development of your children. They will learn to pray for themselves, develop spiritual muscles, and become spiritual giants in their teen years and in adulthood.

Prayer is not meant to be a fisherman's net to trawl and seek the will of God. Instead, we use prayer to pray that God's will can bring us into a place of faith. When we pray, we grow in his will and become confident we are in his will, because our prayers change us to be more like him.

I have often referenced my late grandmother, Peris Wanjiku, who entered eternal rest while I was writing this book. She instilled in my family and me the importance of prayer.

My maternal grandmother, Rahab Wairimu, was no different. She prayed scriptures and talked to God intimately.

As I grew up, visiting my grandmother near the Gura River was a getaway, and a sleepover in her house needed no alarm because at 3:00 a.m., the chicken woke us up. Little did I know or understand that was her alarm clock, and it helped manage my grandmother's daily devotions to prayer,

My last visit with Grandma Peris, fondly known by many as WaKarite, was indeed a curious moment. "How can you explain your parenting of nine children with different lifestyles?"

I asked her. She answered with an attitude of gratitude despite the many challenges of her parental journey. She had to bury half of her children, contrary to God's Word and expectation. But she lived through the tragedy with grace and exhibited Christlike of perseverance and patience, and she grieved with hope. Later in the day, she would find time to read the Bible with my grandfather on their wooden rocking chairs

She clung to and lived out her life based on Paul's word in the book of Philippians: "Do not be anxious about anything, but in every situation, by prayer and petition, with thanksgiving, present your requests to God. And the peace of God that transcends all understanding will guard your hearts and minds in Christ Jesus" (Philippians 4:6–8). I can attest I witnessed a contended grandma, and I never exhibited anxiety from her.

First Thessalonians 5:16–19 had never been so real to her. She recited it again like poetry. "Rejoice always, pray continually, give thanks in all circumstances; for this is God's will for you in Christ Jesus. Do not quench the spirit." The hunger for a personal experience with God and the morning prayers satisfied a committed relationship with the Father. Her prayers were so intimate to God. She would always say, "And now, my Father ..." "Something else, my Father ..." "You are God eternal, the giver of food, life, and everything. Amen!"

The Secret

I learned the secret. You must seek God in the morning if you want him and his presence and guidance through the day. In the previous chapter on grace-abounding parenting, I highlighted that we have a calling to be ambassadors of Christ in our parenting journey. As ambassadors, our resources come from a higher authority: God, his Word, and all his help keeps us operational in an alien world. We are aliens of this world and citizens of heaven. In the book of Colossians, the prison epistle written by Apostle Paul states "Continue steadfastly in prayer, being watchful in it with thanksgiving" (Colossians 4:2).

Praying According to What God Says about Your Child

For a long time, even with my grandmother's experience, the Lord's prayer was a favorite, and I almost recited it by heart. According to his Word, the focus was more on the immediate need than praying to God. The book of James teaches on the prayers of the righteous: "Therefore, confess your sins to one another and pray for one another, that you may be healed. The prayer of a righteous person has great power as it is working" (James 5:6).

Believing Prayer

> Ask, and it will be given to you; seek, and you will find; knock, and it will be opened to you. For everyone who asks receives, and the one who seeks finds, and to the one who knocks it will be opened. (Matthew 7:7–8)

> If you believe, you will receive whatever you ask for in prayer. (Matthew 21:22)

Note that not all asking is really praying, and therefore not all asking will receive. James 4:3 says, "You ask and do not receive, because you ask wrongly, to spend it on your passions." For emphasis, the psalmist says, "If I had cherished iniquity in my heart, the Lord would not have listened. But truly God has listened; he has attended to the voice of my prayer" (Psalm 66:18–19).

Here are at least two kinds of asking that will not bring an answer. Then there are conditions. One is that we must ask in Christ's name. That implies that we believe in Christ as our Savior and are his faithful friends, and therefore we have a right to use his name. This condition narrows down the promise to the loyal followers of Christ.

Another condition is that we are abiding in Christ, and his words are abiding in us. Even a Christian who is following from afar does not come within the circle of this promise. Another qualification that belongs to all promises to prayer: God himself must be the judge as to the things we ask and whether they would be blessings to us. There may be things we desire very earnestly, but it would be the greatest unkindness to grant us. Is God then bound by this promise to give us what we crave? By no means. The Lord will provide what is right. "For the LORD God is a sun and shield, the LORD bestows favor and honor. No good thing does he withhold from those who walk uprightly" (Psalm 84:11). He will withhold even from the most upright the things which in his divine wisdom he sees would not be good things. This is implied in every such promise.

The Tremendous Power of Prayer for a Weary Parent

In rueful admission of emotional and physical weariness, there were countless times I did not wake up saying, "Hallelujah." In Matthew 26:4, Jesus tells his disciples, "Watch and pray, that ye enter not into temptation: the spirit indeed is willing, but the flesh is weak." You may agree with me that you would like to undertake something as a parent, but you lack the energy or strength to do so. God does call you to daily commitment to pray for your children and family. Eventually we have to graduate from praying against the wind to rebuking the wind. As a kingdom child, you have the power and authority to do so, as noted by Paul: "I also pray that you will understand the incredible greatness of God's power for us who believe him. This is the same mighty power that raised Christ from the dead and seated him in the place of honor at God's right hand in the heavenly realms" (Ephesians 1:19–20).

Daily Plugging Into

As parents, our daily schedules fills up a calendar. Every waking moment should be lived in an awareness that God is with us and is actively involved and engaged in our thoughts and actions. We should not be ignorant that we are in a battlefield with Satan and his army, and one of our undeniable weapon is prayer. It is a means of plugging into God's power. In Colossians 4:2, Apostle Paul urges us, "Devote yourselves to prayer with an alert mind and thankful heart."

Prayer for Wisdom

Solomon asked God for wisdom: "Give me an understanding heart." Have wisdom to understand what your purpose is for your children. Don't rush them before God does a good job in them and accomplishes his goal in them. Be a man and woman of prayer. Develop your heart and your skills as a mentor. Be aware of your weakness and vulnerability. Remember that you are representing God.

Simple, Deep Prayer

Father Lord, I thank you for Jesus Christ. As a parent, may I never seek to rely on my human wisdom, physical strength, or picking and choosing what to trust or believe. Still, to help my unbelief, I trust in you, Jesus Christ, knowing that you are all wisdom, might, majesty, dominion, power, strength, love, and life. In Jesus's name, I pray. Amen.

Set Apart unto God

Faith in God is all you need. A false sense of security, economic success, military power, financial bailouts, and political alliances will not save us. I am not ashamed of the gospel because it is the power of God that brings salvation to everyone who believes, first to the Jew and then to the Gentile. For in the gospel, the righteousness of God is revealed—a character that is by faith from first to last, just as it is written: "The righteous shall live by faith" (Romans 1:17).

Faith is knowing that God can do all things, even when you can't see him. Hope believes in God to take the bad away, even when you are beaten down with ongoing trials, suffering, and parental storms. Trust is assuming that all things are possible with God; nothing and no one will ever get in the way of you loving and serving God. "But without Faith, it is impossible to please Him, for he who comes to God must believe that He is and that He is a rewarder of those who diligently seek Him" (Hebrews 11:6). Do you know what pleases God? He's not impressed by how much knowledge we have. He isn't influenced by how many possessions we own. Our accomplishments do not move him. He is driven simply by our faith in him. Ephesians 2:4–8 states, "But because of his great love for us, God, who is rich in mercy, made us alive with Christ even when we were dead in transgressions—it is by grace you have been saved. And God raised us with Christ and seated us with him in the heavenly realms in Christ Jesus, seven so that in the coming ages he might show the incomparable riches of his grace, expressed in his kindness to us in Christ Jesus. For it is by grace you have been saved, through Faith—and this is not from yourselves, it is the gift of God."

Romans 8:29 says, "For whom he foreknew, He also predestined to be conformed to the image of His Son."

Parental storms are pathways that enable you to become more like Jesus. Colossians 4:2 tells us, "Continue earnestly in prayer, be vigilant in it with thanksgiving."

Family Intercessory Prayer

Father, cover this family with your protection. Hide them under your wings. You are the God who forgives all our sins and heals all our diseases. I ask you to cover this sweet little daughter of yours and her entire family with protection and healing. Be their peace and their strength. May they have comfort knowing you can do exceedingly and abundantly above all I (or anyone) can think or ask. You are the great I Am, competent to be the provider of all their needs. God, I invite you to turn your eye and attention toward this family. Supply each need that arises. Thank you for being a good Father, and thank you for your many beautiful promises! I pray these things over them in Jesus's name.

Wailing Mother's Prayer

During the several years of my hospice work, a mother who lost her daughter stated the only way she got some peace was by writing a letter to him and reading it in the morgue. She looked forward to the day she would be joined together with her again, and because her prayers were that before her births she would be a saint, she believed that in death, he became a saint.

It's hard to hold back tears and remember the countless times I have cried, mourned, and grieved with parents. The experiences are traumatizing and emotionally draining to families, and one can only empathize and say, "I know how you feel." Wrong cliché! It is irritating and gives false comfort. No one can feel another's grief. However, you can empathize and mourn with the families, or have a ministry of silence where your presence is more appreciated than words that deepen the bleeding heart.

Praying parents are not immune to trials, suffering, and pain. "I have told you these things so that in me you may have peace. In this world, you will have trouble. But take heart! I have overcome the world" (John 16:33). Both believers and nonbelievers believe that this is the sad reality. The truth remains constant, but our circumstances are uncertain.

Misplaced Prayers

With the understanding and interpretation of prayers, it is important that we pray according to God's Word. What a joy to know there is divine intervention when we go to the Lord in prayer and pray for the perfect will upon our children and the removal of veils from spiritual blindness, as stated by Apostle Paul: "In their case the god of this world has blinded the minds of the unbelievers, to keep them from seeing the light of the gospel of the glory of Christ, who is the image of God" (2 Corinthians 4:4).

But there is warning on misuse of scripture. It is important in your prayers for your children to consider the nature and the challenge at hand. For example, Jesus said, "Have faith in God. Truly, I say to you, whoever says to this mountain, 'Be taken up and thrown into the sea,' and does not doubt in his heart, but believes that what he says will come to pass, it will be done for him. Therefore I tell you, whatever you ask in prayer, believe that you have received it, and it will be yours" (Mark 11:22–24).

Wonderful Truth

Christian leader and pastor James Merritt stated, "The primary purpose of reading the Bible is not to know the Bible but to know God." As parents praying for our children, by reading the Bible we are assured we are praying according to God's will with a right motivation, persistence, and thanksgiving, relying on the spirit of God in prayer. Isn't this a wonderful truth for a parent in pain? "Likewise the Spirit helps us in our weakness. For we do not know what to pray for as we ought, but the Spirit himself intercedes for us with groanings too deep for words. And he who searches hearts knows what is the mind of the Spirit, because the Spirit intercedes for the saints according to the will of God" (Romans 8:26–27). Parents, you are the Bible your child daily reads. As Charles Spurgeon once said, *"Nobody ever outgrows Scripture; the book widens and deepens with our years"* (Charles Spurgeon, *Brilliants*, 1892).

The psalmist cried in Psalm 119:25, "My soul clings to the dust." If you could find the solution within yourself, you would have changed yourself and the pain of your parenting. But you need to look to God! He's the only one with sustaining strength.

The prodigal Parent And The Prodigal Child

American football is played during the week of my birthday, and though my son played high school football at varsity level, the game rules and language used by the reference is far from my comprehension. But there is one lesson learned from the 2018 football season: Never give up. When all hope is lost, in that setback, there is always a comeback!

Many of our children have been fugitives of war, trapped by drugs, alcoholism, phonography, prostitution, gluttony, anger, and many other things. They find themselves trapped in situations and conditions contrary to the will of God, and they have not been able to escape. They are held hostage! It is a sad discovery that churchgoing and praying did not release them either. The prodigal son, after running away from home and living life recklessly and wildly, realized that he didn't deserve a second chance from his father. He thought to himself that when he returned home, he would become one of the hired servants instead of a son. He had not anticipated that his father would welcome him with open arms and restore him to his position. He had thought to himself that his years of wild living and squandering his wealth had ruined his chances of ever being accepted again. "And the son said to him, 'Father, I have sinned against heaven and before you. I am no longer worthy to be called your son.' But the father said to his servants, 'Bring quickly the best robe, and put it on him, and put a ring on his hand, and shoes on his feet. And bring the fattened calf and kill it, and let us eat and celebrate. For this my son was dead, and is alive again; he was lost, and is found.' And they began to celebrate" (Luke 15:21–24). The current situation or distraction in your child's life seems grievous, but God is a God of second chances and endless chances!

The detours and distractions have caused unimaginable mental, emotional, and sometimes physical pain, resulting in bitterness, anger, resentment, and disappointment. We feel the sins of our children deserve no second chance, but God dispenses love to you and your children as a gift. Embrace your children with open arms as they come back to their senses and return to him.

You may feel it's too late to return for that child to turn around to God, or it's too late to pray and ask God for forgiveness- the prodigal parent. You may have a strained parent-child relationship, or a child who ran away from home or from God, despite the love. It's not too late. If there was a prayer a parent in pain can pray, it is for patience and understanding every step of the journey.Bear good patience and wait for your prayers to be answered, and your blessings will be revealed. For the parent wondering if that child hooked on alcohol, drugs, pornography, a different sexual orientation, or homelessness, remember that our God is a God of possibilities. The prodigal shall return.

Dry Bones Shall Live!

I have seen God work for my best interest. No matter the way I felt or saw with my naked eyes, I can attest and encourage you, like Ezekiel 37:4–5, "Prophesy over these bones, and say to them, O dry bones, hear the word of the Lord. Thus says the Lord God to these bones: Behold, I will cause breath to enter you, and you shall live." Ezekiel is ordered by God to prophesy upon the dry bones and to the wind. He preached and prayed, and the dead bones lived by a power that went along with the Word of God that he preached and the prayer that he prayed.

The effectiveness of the word and prayer cannot be emphasized more for the raising of dead souls. "A verse a day to keep the devil away," as my favorite speaker, Priscilla Shirer, would say. You must be earnest with God in prayer for the working of his Word by the power of the Holy Spirit.

"And he said to me, 'Son of man, can these bones live?' And I answered, 'O Lord God, you know'" (Ezekiel 37:3). In that hopeless situation, in the detours over your parenting, you are seeking answers. The Lord has the final say. Yes, he knows.

Sometimes I have a tendency to say a prayer and expect instant answers. I call them microwave expectations. Your persistence in prayer and seeking God over the dead situation is not in vain. It may seem that all hope is gone regarding that addiction, poor choice, rebellion, or whatever. Where there is a setback, there is always a comeback. God, in his infinite mercy, made the fountain of life able to breathe life over your child's situation. Trust him in the journey. Trust that his timing is perfect.

Jesus Christ gave good instructions, and even the withered tree was fruitful. That prodigal son can return! The wayward child can turn around! Jesus taught them to pray in faith:

"Have faith in God" (Mark 11:22). They were in awe of the power of Jesus's command of the word. "Why, Jesus, a lively active faith would put as great a power into your prayers" (Mark 11:23–24). There is assurance of strength and power of God, and the greatest challenge and difficulty in parenting shall be affected. That was the faith of miracles, which the apostles did wonders supernaturally and naturally, healing the sick, raising the dead, casting out devils, and doing many more things equated by Jesus as the removing of mountains. Our spiritual eyes and understanding are required in our journey. "It justifies us" (Romans 5:1). It removes the mountains of waywardness, the detours, and casts them into the depths of the sea. It heals and purifies the heart (Acts 15:9). It restores, and it removes mountains of substance abuse, broken families, different sexual orientation, and poor choices. It "makes them plains" (Zechariah 4:7) by the grace of God.

Truth Be Told

As a mental health coach and biblical counselor, I have come across many falsehoods in our livelihoods, including my own. Many times I have fallen victim to this lie when asked, "How are you, Lucy?" I quickly answer, "Oh, praise God, all is good," yet sometimes I am bleeding on the inside and smiling on the outside. Why is truth not often told? There is nothing we can hide from God.

There is a societal need to open up. It is okay to say you are not okay. Accept these hard truths and brace against the storm barrier.

As I revise this manuscript, I am constantly reminding myself of the need for truth, from the individual level to the corporate level. The lyrics of the song "Truth Be Told" by Matthew West cannot be more appropriate for such a time as this.

Lie number one: You're supposed to have it all together

And when they ask how you're doin', just smile and tell them, "Never better"

Lie number two: Everybody's life is perfect except yours

So keep your messes and your wounds and your secrets safe with you behind closed doors

But truth be told

There's no sin You don't already know

The issues of the heart matter. "Trust in the LORD with all your heart, and lean not unto your understanding. In all thy ways acknowledge him, and he shall direct thy paths" (Proverbs 3:5–6). The scripture is also written for rebuke, so correction must learn the exegesis of scripture and lean not on our feelings, which will not make sense. Faith is our sixth sense. Demanding answers according to our emotions and circumstances is disobedience.

Joseph's Faithfulness When Nothing Made Sense

Many times I told the Lord, "You brought me from far country, miles and miles away, to a land of milk and honey. I saw the grapes like Joshua and Caleb after nights of vigil. But now the brook is dry, and I no longer see the grapes in my parenting."

I was reminded of Joseph's life. His puzzle was not complete, yet every step of the way, he trusted. A good example is Elijah, when nothing made sense: "And after a while, the brook dried up, because there was no rain in the land" (1 Kings 17:7).

There is a clear indication from a biblical perspective. Your joy and freedom as a believer in the Lord Jesus are not in so many things sought after, such as riches and reaching the pinnacle of your career. The truth is that God intends you to find your identity and self-worth in Jesus Christ alone. Did you know you are a saint? Brother Paul clearly indicates this in Ephesians 2:19, "So then you are no longer strangers and aliens, but you are fellow citizens with the saints and members of the household of God. Ephesians 3:17–18 states, "So that Christ may dwell in your hearts through faith—that you, being rooted and grounded in love, may have strength to comprehend with all the saints what is the breadth and length and height and depth."

The daily affirmation and belief that God's promises are true rejuvenate and recharge you. You are heard! When connected to God through Jesus Christ, you can freely express your emotions and thoughts, and you can answer according to his will. "Then you will call upon me and come and pray to me, and I will hear you. You will seek me and find me, when you seek me with all your heart" (Jeremiah 29:12). With this revelation as a parent, the fragrance of Christ can spread to your children and your family.

In Need of Advice and Prayer

I received this piece from a parent.

> I have been praying for my young adult daughter for over ten years, but she will not stop. She recently stole over twenty-one thousand dollars from the family's bank accounts, and even her grandfather after he passed. It is to the point where it has come down to pressing charges, and hopefully when all is said and done, if she is still alive when the warrant is issued and they find her, she goes to court. It has taken its toll.

She has given up on her handsome little boy, who lives with her grandparents. Her family has given a lot over years of trying to help, but all is manipulated and taken advantage of. I have to find the strength to let it go, learn from her own mistakes, pray for restoration and healing, and hope that I see the transformation one day. However, for now, it is distance, and I can do no more enabling. I have tried to look at it from her side, but after she stole over twenty-one thousand dollars from an elderly person who lives on government assistance, she can no longer be tolerated. I pray she makes it. Nevertheless, she needs to be accountable for her decisions and choices. This act was the last straw. Please advise!

Tough Love

There is no distance to the spirit. Physical touch or connection may not be possible, and the phone is off, or you have no contact. You feel disabled. My dear friend, don't be manipulated. Keep praying for her! Keep praying for him! Persistent, fervent prayer does move mountains. Storm the gates of heaven with prayers. Stay strong. I know it is easier said than done, but you love her or him, and she or he knows that.

Everything our adult children do is by their own choices. Remember the earlier discussion of sin and its consequences. There are greater forces within them that bring about the detours, as stated by one of my favorites authors, Paul Tripp, in his book *Parenting*: "The foolishness inside your children is more dangerous to them than the temptation outside of them. Only God's power has the power to rescue fools!"

You may say, "Lucy, are you depicting my child as a fool?" Let us examine the scriptures that have the final authority.

Some rebuke, and teaching may be the best dosage now. Apostle Paul wrote in 2 Timothy 3:16–17, "All scripture is breathed out by God and is profitable for teaching, for reproof, for correction, and for training in righteousness that the man of God may be complete, equipped for every good work."

Where does the foolishness of our children come from? Is it even biblical? Absolutely, yes. It is as we saw in the beginning, in the Garden of Eden. It is not what they say or do, or who they are or will become. Unfortunately, they were born with it. They sin and cannot save themselves, and they need a Savior to rescue them. The book of Proverbs is explicit regarding the words of wisdom from a father to his son: "Keep your heart with all vigilance for from it flow the springs of life!" (Proverbs 4:23).

Maybe it is a good time to have that heart-focused conversation with those wayward children. You will have no choice but to embrace them with unconditional love. Pray and never stop getting it to God. In the end, they have to decide to go into recovery and stick with it. Only they can do that. By always helping, you are only enabling. The sooner they hit rock bottom, the sooner they can get help, but they have to want it. The only thing you can do is let go and let God.

Understanding the Stronghold of Substance Abuse

Here is a success story as narrated by Dickson, an overcomer.

> Addiction? Such an ugly word. I am over three decades clean today. There is nothing you can do or say that will make them stop. They alone have to want to stop. Drugs take you to a different world all your own, another dimension of your own where you are not feeling anything; you are safe from reality. I used for fifteen years; the only reason I stopped? I remember thinking it's like living in your nightmares, and dope will turn

it around, and you are once again living in your dreams—a world all your own. But in reality, I was living on the railroad tracks for eight years. I lived on the streets. I thought it was cool. Then you wake up dope sick. That's the worst feeling in the world. I asked, Why am I here? Why do I live like this? The horror that you left your children behind for what bombards your mind, heart, and soul. You're broken. Time to go back to my dreams. And it played over and over again.

One time I was so tired of the nightmares, I fell to my knees and said, God, help me. I used heroin, cocaine, and crack cocaine sometimes. That week I had gotten a massive abscess on my right thigh, and it busted open. It was ugly and it hurt, but we addicts improvise, taking penicillin to get at the hole-in-the-wall stores. Peroxide and alcohol were not strangers.

I am still out there in those streets. Gotta get my money. Cannot be sick. It got to the point where my man was pushing me around in a shopping cart. One day we got our dope and went to an alley to use. I fell over, could not feel my legs and arms, and couldn't walk. I was taken to the hospital, and sepsis had invaded my bloodstream. I was anemic and malnourished. I was on the verge of death!

I remember with fondness the day I cried out to God and had a Damascus experience, and I saw the light that transformed me from Saul to Paul. I asked God to forgive me and said that I didn't want to live this way. My kids would come over and help me. I told God, If you will allow me to

> walk and get my strength back throughout my body, Lord, I will never use drugs again. When you are a drug addict in the hospital, they do not treat you like other people. They treat you like an enemy: you did this to yourself. I know—I've seen it, heard it, and got no help from anyone but my God.
>
> I lost many friends due to drug addiction. It hurts. The change had to start with my acceptance that I needed the transformation. I know I asked God for help, but also the prayers of my burden bearers, and he stopped me in my tracks. It was a long and painful recovery. I give God all the glory and pray for those lost and blinded by addictions and wrong choices. Do not give up. God is able and is no respecter of persons! What he did for me, he can do for you!

How can God be good and powerful, yet there is a collapsing economy, injustice, a food shortage, and pandemic? Children get lost in various ways in the storms of life. God has spoken to our hearts and drawn us to his presence. Studying and listening to God brings reconciliation of two worlds: the world of God's truth and the world of man's mind. The flesh wages war against the spirit, but by the power of the Holy Spirit, we overcome. No matter the situation with your child, dear friend, squeeze those scriptures like oranges, meditate on the Word, and pray until the Holy Spirit becomes a part of your bloodstream.

Here is a parent's prayer for children: You may give thanks always. You will be aligned with God's will. You may walk in a manner worthy of the Lord. You may bear fruit in every good work. You may increase, be strengthened, and be sustained with the power of God. You may pray continually, as in 1 Thessalonians 5:17.

Everlasting God in the Lives of Our Children

Raise a child who prays. "Mom, I want to pray like you," my teenage daughter said one day. That lit a bulb in my spirit, to know the understanding of my daughter on prayer. Did I assume she knew about prayer? Yes, and it was wrong assumption!

In a society that is abandoning biblical principles and in a culture where prayer is not popular for Generation Z, you parents have a task to create this culture in your home. Nurture and develop it! How do you help them pray like Jesus? Pray effectively from a young age.

My discussion with my daughter on prayer directed me to Matthew 6, on the Lord's instruction.

> And when you pray, you must not be like the hypocrites. For they love to stand and pray in the synagogues and at the street corners, that they may be seen by others. Truly, I say to you, they have received their reward. But when you pray, go into your room and shut the door and pray to your Father who is in secret. And your Father who sees in secret will reward you.
>
> And when you pray, do not heap up empty phrases as the Gentiles do, for they think that they will be heard for their many words. Do not be like them, for your Father knows what you need before you ask him. (Matthew 6:5–8)

My teachable moments in my daughter's question is that there is no fanciness in prayer. In prayer, your communication from your heart is what God is more interested in, rather than particular words you use.

I remember with fondness in my early walk with Christ, I was in a large outdoor public Christian fellowship in my mother country, Kenya. At what is referred as the "crusades" one evangelist denounced poetical prayers. This resonates with my childhood memories: every time we embarked on a road trip, there was a particular prayer. "O Lord we pray for the cars that have been made with man's hands." There is nothing wrong in praying for God's protection, however you are to pour your heart to God and not simply recite memorized words.

Our children can learn persistence and resilience in prayer through watching us pray, but God requires their sincere communication and pouring of their hearts.

Soldier in the Army

As mentioned in other chapters, there is need for a daily commitment to guidance, protection, and wisdom regarding living day-to-day life and applying God's law. What follows are God's instructions from holy scriptures: **"You then, my child, be strengthened by the grace that is in Christ Jesus, and what you have heard from me in the presence of many witnesses entrust to faithful men, who will be able to teach others also. in suffering as a good soldier of Christ Jesus. No soldier gets entangled in civilian pursuits, since his aim is to please the one who enlisted him" (2 Timothy 2:1–4).**

Beyond You but Possible with God

Only in those moments when you realize that these things are genuinely outside your control will your prayer and your faith in God have a chance to operate and propel you forward.

"Be joyful in hope, patient in affliction, faithful in prayer"(Romans 12:12). "And the peace of God, which surpasses all understanding, will guard your hearts and your minds as you live in Christ Jesus" (Philippians 4:7).

James 1:2–3 encourages us by saying, "Count it all, the joy my brothers, when you meet trials of various kinds, for you know that the testing of your faith produces steadfastness." When Elijah told Ahab that it was about to rain, it was not because he saw any physical evidence that suggested that rain was on the way. There were no dark clouds; there were no television weather reports. There were no meteorologists and no cell phones to check the weather forecast. He said it would rain because God had told him that it would not rain again unless Elijah commanded the drought to come to an end. Elijah said what he said in faith; he spoke the things that are not as though they were. And true to his word, the rain did come.

Where am I going with this? We can believe that faith uses a different pair of eyes. Even when all the physical evidence around you suggests otherwise, religion focuses on the unseen things. Elijah was exercising his faith when he said it would rain, although it may have been a sunny day. He fixed his eyes above, on God, and trusted the word that God had given him. How many of us speak the things that are not as though they are? Do we go with what we see in the physical or what is unseen in the spiritual? Do we go with what our circumstances tell us? Or do we go with what God said concerning our children?

It may look like your family is falling apart when your child is acting contrary to your expectations. Where do you fix your eyes—on your child's behavior, or on the promise of God? It may look like your child has been written off and will never be able to get off the addiction when you look at the level of dependence on substance abuse or suffering. Your family, friends, and community have written off your child. Your child has become the reference of that drunkard son or daughter, that naughty boy, that homeless one, that disabled person ... the list is endless.

Yet you received a prophecy that said your child should be delivered, and the prodigal one shall return. As parents, we fix our eyes on the promises of God. It may look like your child's health situation will never change, yet the Lord promised you healing. Do you continue to speak about the change you are waiting for, or does your confession change to what you can see?

Remember, no trouble is too tangled for God to untie. No path is too twisted for him to straighten. No heart is again shattered for him to gather up and put back together.

Your problems may be bewildering, but your God is wise. He sees you. He knows every detail of your trouble. And he knows how to come alongside you as you wait for him and make you rise with wings like eagles.

When you are weak, God wants you to be vital for you. He wants to be the rock you lean on, the strong tower that you run to. Overwhelming times shows us God is the source of our strength.

Your problems may be significant, perhaps even bigger than you know. But your God is bigger, and His promises to you are more robust and surer. Therefore look up from your problems. Listen again to God's powerful, wise counsel. And then ask God to help you behold him.

Trust God! God's unsteadfast love is with you at all times.

The Manifestation of God's Word

Hannah was barren, but I think what made her feel the barrenness even more was she had a tormenting spirit unleashed against her life by the name of Peninnah. This woman found joy in ridiculing Hannah and making fun of her barrenness. She was determined to make Hannah's life miserable, and for a while she succeeded. But what she had not anticipated was Hannah's response. She had not expected that Hannah would take her pain and place it in the hands of the Lord.

Hannah prayed in such a controversial way when she went before the altar. That manner of praying even had Eli, the priest, confused, thinking Hannah was drunk on wine. He hadn't known that there are moments in life where you have no choice but to pray like a madwoman. Eli had not known that rock bottom would push one to realms in the spirit that one had never known were possible. Hannah had gotten to that point where she was sick and tired and needed intervention.

Hannah's pain caused her to focus on her barrenness. For that very season, when she was down to nothing, she birthed what would later become one of the greatest prophets. Hannah birthed a miracle! Sometimes your enemies don't even know that they are pushing you into destiny. They have no idea that the pain they are causing you will cause you to evolve and manifest. These people don't know that they are pushing you to birth a miracle.

Are you facing intense pain and or criticism? Are there barren areas in your child's life that you are repeatedly being mocked for? The best revenge is to focus on God's Word. Surround yourself with burden bearers. Don't pick up the same stones and throw them back. Let your pain push you closer to the Lord. Let your pain get you to worship God in unconventional ways. Let your rock-bottom days move you to mountaintops. Work on that vision, work on that goal, work on that idea that God has given you. God has your child's future in his hands!

Praying Scripture and Teachings over Your Child

> My son, keep your Father's commandments and forsake not your mother's teaching. (Proverbs 6:20)

> Bind them on your heart, always tie them around your neck. (Proverbs 6:21)

> When you walk, they will guide you; when you sleep, they will watch over you; when you awake, they will speak to you. (Proverbs 6:22)

> For these commands are a lamp, this teaching is a light, and the corrections of discipline are the way to live. (Proverbs 6:23)

> I have been reminded of your sincere faith, which first lived in your grandmother Lois and your mother Eunice and, I am persuaded, now lives in you also. (2 Timothy 1:5)

As written by Apostle Paul, these women had a responsibility of passing on their faith to the next generation. What will you pass to your next generation?

10

~~*~~

The DNA of God's Steadfast Love

> Just like a tree, the roots must be set deeply in place before the trunk, branches and fruit can grow.
>
> —Anonymous

Foundation of Steadfast Love

As I mentioned earlier, I wrote this book in the middle of the COVID-19 pandemic I witnessed that tragedy transforms, but there is pain in purpose. I wrote a book and found a hobby of planting flowers. In late summer 2020, my family enjoyed planting various flowers, herbs, and trees. Watching the garden flourish is a joy. Digging deep into the soil is not my favorite, but it is necessary to allow the roots to deepen. This analogy can be linked to the steadfast love of God that cuts deep our relationship with God and our children, no matter the detours or the stormy journey!

My fellow parents, as we come close to the final discussions regarding our vitally important parenting journey, Apostle Paul reminds us in 2 Timothy 1:13, "Follow the pattern of the sound words that you have heard from me, in the Faith and the love that are in Christ Jesus. Abide In His Love."

For many years I struggled with the meaning of love and equated it to feelings. In times of offense, I let the emotions rule and did not display the fruit of the spirit. The realization that love is a commitment no matter the season makes life more palatable. In times of storms and detours, there it can be a challenge to mirror that love, but in obedience we have no choice but to love them no matter the circumstance. The garden must be nurtured, sometimes pruning for better fruits. The same is true of our relationships: give steadfast love, nurture them, and solidify them with much growth.

"But I gave my child a firm foundation," you say. That foundation is a strong root to your relationship before the branches and fruits are evident. They will weather through the storms. It may take days, months, or decades, which is a hard reality. But remember what is written in the second epistle of Peter: "But do not overlook this one fact, beloved, that with the Lord one day is as a thousand years, and a thousand years as one day" (2 Peter 3:8).

To the human mind, there is a huge difference between one day and a thousand years, but to God there is no difference. He is all-knowing of the present, past, and future. In our longsuffering during our journey, he calls us to abound in grace and good works, and to bring him glory and for our good.

Do you not know what to do with the poor choices warranting tough love? We have unveiled the ambassadorial parental role, and no doubt our parental relationship is equated to the unwavering love God has toward us, including his acceptance, mercy, and trust. His unfailing love is always available.

Do you wonder why the world feels scarier than ever? I think we are more and more exhausted as circumstances seem impossible. Self-reliance is no more my go-to. We can abide in him, as stated in 1 John 4:16, "So we have come to know and to believe the love that God has for us. God is love, and whoever abides in love abides in God, and God abides in him."

Christian Maturity

The parental season of pain and suffering was not without explanation and benefit for me. It was a season of growth that shaped me. Truth be told, some seasons have softened me and caused me to evaluate my parental styles. Do you wake up with a weight on your shoulders for what you see around you? The comfort of scriptures is a brook in your dry spell. Lamentations 3:22–23 states, "The steadfast love of the LORD never ceases; his mercies never come to an end; they are new every morning; great is your faithfulness."

The latter years of parenting were more glorious and joyful, with occasional storms, but I must say and confess, "But God" (Ephesians 2:4). Intentionally strive toward Christian maturity. There is nothing to be shy about, and Paul states,

> If I speak in the tongues of men and angels but have not love, I am a noisy gong or a clanging cymbal. And if I have prophetic powers, and understand all mysteries and all knowledge, and if I have all faith, so as to remove mountains, but have not love, I am nothing. If I give away all I have, and if I deliver up my body to be burned, but have not love, I gain nothing.

> Love is patient and kind; love does not envy or boast; it is not arrogant or rude. It does not insist on its own way; it is not irritable or resentful; it does not rejoice at wrongdoing but rejoices with the truth. Love bears all things, believes all things, hopes all things, endures all things. (1 Corinthians 13:1–8)

Your Home A Haven Of Laughter And Joy

Apostle Paul points us to the process of becoming and conforming to the image of Christ. The same could be applied to our children. A sacrificial type of love is called for, and has a transformative effect on both the child and parent.

> Love never ends. When I was a child, I spoke like a child, I thought like a child, I reasoned like a child. When I became a man, I gave up childish ways. For now, we see in a mirror dimly but then face to face. Now I know in part; then I shall know fully, even as I have been fully known. So now Faith, hope, and love abide, these three; but the greatest of these is love. (1 Corinthians 13:8–13)

What is your excuse? Your feelings will fail you. Love is a commitment, and better still it is a thoughtful decision. The transformative power leads toward growth and a better relationship, and a home becomes a haven of laughter and joy.

The stormy season allowed me to experience God's comfort, compassion, and growth. The waiting room is not a fun place to be alone, but with the Lord on our side, no one can be against us! The power of praise while waiting makes the journey bearable. One of my favorite hymns is by Louisa M. R. Stead: "How Sweet It Is to Trust in Jesus."

> It is so sweet to trust in Jesus,
> Just to take Him at His Word
> Just to rest upon His promise,
> Just to know, "Thus saith the Lord!"
> Jesus, Jesus, how I trust Him!
> How I've proved Him o'er and o'er

Can I Disagree with My Children and Still Love Them?

It is important to remember that you are not always going to agree with your children in their detours. Disagreement can eat away at your patience. Learn how to have a conversation and still maintain loving relationships with your children. There is no better summary of Christian growth and maturity than the commands of our Lord Jesus Christ in 1 John 4:8, "Anyone who does not love does not know God, because God is love."

Trusting or Trucking God

My daughter is the master tracker of her goods, especially shoes. Goods from Amazon arrive pretty fast, but shoes from other companies get delayed, and she has to keep tracking them. When she reads they are in transit, she gets excited. The actual arrival of the shoe is met with sheer joy.

Would it be the same for tracking God and his promises? No. But he can be trusted even when we cannot track him. He is not in transit. He lives within us. He is "Immanuel" **(Matthew 1:23),** meaning God is with us. He cares, and we can trust him to do an excellent job in our lives and the lives of our families.

He is comfortable, no matter how unstable you have been. He is stable and remains the same. His purpose is fixed. Rest in his promises. He is the rock on which we fix our feet in the valley on the dry bones. His permanence of character guarantees the fulfillment of his promises. His love is steadfast. Let us spread the fragrance of his love to our own, even when it hurts. "For the mountains shall depart, and the hills are removed, but My steadfast love shall not depart from you and my covenant of my peace shall not be removed, says the Lord who has compassion on you" (Isaiah 54:10).

My fellow parents, we were not designed to carry the weight of being God. Let us remind our hearts that God is good at being God. Moreover, we can trust him at all times. That is why he gave his one and only Son to be the Savior of the world!

It is okay to feel hurt and confused about situations in your life. "Lucy, did you say it is okay to feel hurt?" Yes! But do not let your feelings lead you away from God or away from his truth. When it feels like all that is left of your heart and your story is broken pieces, you can bring them all to God. He is big enough to handle our honest feelings. He is not afraid of our doubts or our questions. Furthermore, his truth will not leave us, even when our gut cries do not sound so Christian.

Let us press into him in those very places where we may feel tempted to pull away. Let us ask him to meet us and speak to us in the pages of his Word. Let us remember that it is better to wrestle with truth than to stay stuck in our places of turmoil.

The Power of Love and Prayer

Let us continue to pray, and by the power of the Holy Spirit, we shall overcome. Do not throw in the towel because Satan will deceive you. Remember that he is a master killer, thief, and destroyer. But what a joy to know that God is the sole author of our lives and our children's lives! Jesus has given us life, and this parental journey is filled with abundance. The power of love and prayer will carry us through.

Therefore be full of faith, holding fast to God's promises and moving forward into that future with God. May your faithfulness shine forth as an example for others and our children that we too may prove faithful. Proverbs 13:22 reminds us, "A good man leaves an inheritance to his children's children." What is your legacy or inheritance? Will you live for your children? Is it wealth or spiritual investment, or both?

The Name of Jesus

According to Hebrew culture, a man's name referred to his authority and reputation. In the same way, the Word of God and the phrases of Jesus refer to his power and prominence. That is why today we pray in the name of Jesus Christ, "Whatever you ask in my name, this I will do, that the Father may be glorified in the Son. If you ask me anything in my name, I will do it" (John 14:13). John 16:23–24 states, "In that day you will ask nothing of me. Truly, truly, I say to you, whatever you ask of the Father in my name, he will give it to you. Until now you have asked nothing in my name. Ask, and you will receive, that your joy may be full." We pray according to his authority, and we command healing in the name of Jesus Christ. "But Peter said, 'I have no silver and gold, but what I do have I give to you. In the name of Jesus Christ of Nazareth, rise up and walk!'" (Acts 3:6). Why must demons come out when we use the name of Jesus Christ? "And this she kept doing for many days. Paul, having become greatly annoyed, turned and said to the spirit, ;I command you in the name of Jesus Christ to come out of her;" (Acts 16:18). Why was baptism done in the name of Jesus Christ? "And he commanded them to be baptized in the name of Jesus Christ" (Acts 10:48).

A clear explanation is that God's name was his authority and reputation, so a cultural understanding of this translation is that God exalted his Word above all other things that are under his control, even his jurisdiction. "For you have upgraded your Word above all your name" (Psalm 138:2). God's Word and authority are exalted above all creation, and that is undoubtedly true. God has exalted his Word above his power and lives by his own rules. Therefore he can be trusted to keep his promises.

The only real constant and the only thing that truly makes any sense in the parenting journey is God. By now you realize praise plays a big role in my journey! Singing and praising my journey transforms the atmosphere. I have seen this Jesus. Embrace him in your parenting journey. Praise him with songs.

I echo the words and lyrics of Casting Crowns: "Love them like Jesus, carry them to him." A solid foundation is one of the most important things parents need to create in the relationships with their children.

11

Becoming Perfectly Imperfect

> Recognizing what you are unable to do is essential to good parenting
> —Paul Tripp

When my sons were eighteen years old, I was ready to hit the hallelujah exit button and do a victory dance. Wrong, Ms. Lucy! I remember with fondness my mother telling me, "You will always be my Shiru," an assurance of her parental support despite my rebellion. Her shortcomings, imperfections, and spiritual legacy lives on after her painful departure home to the Lord.

I finally want to craft a story of a perfect parent with perfect children. I sometimes wish I could delete parts of my parental journey, but that would omit the beauty of it all and my trusting God in hard realities and fun times!Tears and Joy! Sometimes our messiness, craziness, dysfunction, getting real with one another, and the fragrance of love no matter what is the glue that keeps us together.

There are many stages in a child's life from infancy to adulthood with many dimensions. As a parent, you learn them as you journey through an experiential experience! They have inner needs, they need individual freedoms, they build character into their hearts, and finally they can find true greatness, which includes an unquenchable love for Christ and others. Diversion of such truths leads to poor choices and consequences, but giving children the freedom to make mistakes creates an atmosphere of grace. Did I say mistakes? Yes. We are reminded in the Acts 17:30 of the apostles that "the times of ignorance God overlooked, but now he commands all people everywhere to repent?"

Our children do not need the gospel more than we do. They need it differently than we do. As parents, we sin and fall short. The nightmare came regarding how to nurture adult children while encouraging their independence in college and then in their careers. As I mentioned in the last chapter, there is no how-to magic button in parenting, but each parent and child has unique sets of problems and challenges. The answers may not be obvious, but God's grace is sufficient to parent through the years of ignorance. Let us continue to pray and ask for redeeming grace.

Keep in mind that parenting is a journey, not a destination. We learn and grow in the process with no expectation of perfection. Is the journey one-way? No. Our children may sometimes seem distant, but they are part and parcel of the journey, as Paul states in Ephesians 4:15, "Rather, speaking the truth in love, we are to grow up in every way into him who is the head, into Christ."

Tears Are Healthy

There is nothing wrong with tears. Jesus wept, and he was perfect in every way. Most of our earthly tears come from sorrow, grief, loneliness, and heartache. The emotional pain can be unfathomable, but we always have to reference and know who we are, "and to be renewed in the spirit of your minds" (Ephesians 4:23).

Nevertheless, there will be no such experiences in heaven. Imagine a home with no adverse experiences—ever! That is heaven, and that is our home. In the meantime, let us make our homes his representatives. "We are ambassadors for Christ, God making his appeal through us" (2 Corinthians 5:20). "No discipline seems pleasant at the time but painful. Later on, however, it produces a harvest of righteousness and peace for those trained by it" (Hebrews 12:11).

Children's Choice

When I was growing up, my choices were secondary to my well-meaning parents. Did it always work well? Absolutely not, but wishing for what could have been does no good. The choice to do better for my children is beneficial to my children and family.

Well-known American author and pastor A. W. Tozer once talked about responsibility of choice in reference to the young ruler. Our Lord Jesus looked at him as he walked away. He did not coerce him in any way or follow him.

> The dignity of the young man's humanity forbade that his choices should be made for him by another. To remain a man he must make his own moral choices.
>
> —A. W. Tozer

As Tozer further explains, Jesus knew about the man's choices and permitted him to make the choice, If his human choice took him at last to hell, at least he went there a man. It is better for the moral universe that he should do so rather than he should be jockeyed to a heaven he did not choose as a soulless, will-less automaton.

God takes ninety-nine steps toward us and our children, but he will not take the hundredth. In his infinite mercies, he gives us free will to repent, but he cannot coerce us or our children to repent. God bestows his gift upon us, but the nature of sin and righteousness are voluntary, and both have consequences. God wants us and our children to repent, making a complete change of direction toward him. If not, it results in spiritual and physical death. We have discussed extensively sin and its consequences. As Paul states in Romans 6:23, "For the wages of sin is death, but the free gift of God is eternal life in Christ Jesus our Lord."

Parents, embrace what your children's hearts yearn for—without a parent's guilt. That negative feeling comes from not doing things a certain way, doing them too much, or doing them wrong according to some unknowable and ever-changing rulebook. Advise them positively in their pursuit of joy and a blessed future.

From a certain age, they are the drivers of their lives, and as a senior driver, the best you can do is guide them and not grab the steering wheel from their hands. God has established choices. Sovereignty involves choice too. He gives us the option of good or evil that the gist of humanity but, he gives us freedom to not live like robots. God creates choice, which allows for evil or good. If our children choose evil, then they suffer the consequences. If they choose to repent or turn around, God is merciful. God allows things that reveal detours and sin. Rebellion allows the character of God to be revealed.

Loving Your Child on Purpose

I know that how I react in times of adversity is a clear indication of my heart's state. I have one of two reactions in those moments. First, peace that I can overcome and trust in God's provision. Second, anger that fills my mind with doubt and causes me to react or speak negatively. I realize in those times the truth of what lies beyond the surface. It gives credence to the phrases "When the rubber meets the road" and "You find out what you are made of." In those moments, we must choose to deal with what has been made clear to us. Otherwise, we risk allowing ourselves to be misled, and that can cause a stumbling block to our growth in our walk with God.

Second Corinthians 3:17 clearly indicates, "Now the Lord is the Spirit, and where the Spirit of the Lord is, there is freedom." God gives us freedom of choice, and now we are living lives led by the Spirit. Parental control has its place if done lovingly. As we let our children have the freedom of choice, they will be good managers of their lives. Will they make mistakes? Definitely. These are inevitable, teachable moments of life to grow their character and build resilience, endurance, and confidence.

There is a strong connection between what's in your heart and the words you speak. I believe the two go hand in hand. It seems we should examine our hearts more closely and more regularly. The issues we have never arise when things are going well. But when things are challenging or difficult, we find out what is secretly hiding in those places of our hearts that affect what we speak or how we react. As believers, we live out and speak from what lies within our hearts. We might be able to talk for a while, but eventually the truth is revealed and testifies to what is truly going on.

Our words have power, and we use them daily to communicate things to others that can have a powerful impact on their wellbeing or break them down, as written in Proverbs 18:21, "Death and life are in the power of the tongue, and those who love it will eat its fruits."

Parents, use this scripture to examine and make sure your words line up with your hearts. Otherwise, we are lying to ourselves, to our children, to our families, and most important to God. Jesus said. "The thief comes only to steal and kill and destroy. I came that they may have life and have it abundantly" (John 10:10). This is a promise we can live a life of abundance and bring hope. The and the gifts God has entrusted in you will alleviate family struggles.

Here is an example prayer:

> Lord, may You increase as I decrease in my parenting endeavors. I want to calmly and peacefully choose the paths you want me to take. In Jesus's name, Amen!
>
> Let the peace of Christ rule in my heart since you have called me to peace as your vessel and Ambassador and I am eternally thankful. (Colossians 3:15)
>
> Let the words of my mouth and the meditation of my heart be acceptable in thy sight, O Lord, my strength, and my redeemer. (Psalm 19:14)

Choose to love the children as you shape and mold their lives for eternity.

Forgiveness

Along the parental journey, some seasons have thorns and thistles, but sometimes thorns have roses. In times of pain, there is a war waging in the response. Many times my flesh wages against the spirit, and it is a good time to be aware of of the biblical knowledge and allow it to illuminate you hearts !No doubt forgiveness and steadfast love is found!

Sunday mornings, my faith is really tested to get to church on time and get four children in the car—assuming they even wake up! A friend once asked, "Lucy, don't you think Satan has some minions to distract us?" Yes, the enemy uses our weakness to take away the joy of the Master. But as Paul would say, "And have put on the new self, which is being renewed in knowledge after the image of its creator" (Colossians 3:10). Make your faith credible to your child.

In the pain and heartaches, forgiveness eases the journey. Healing and restoration of the family due to God's compassion is evident. Romans 2:4 states, "Or do you presume on the riches of his kindness and forbearance and patience, not knowing that God's kindness is meant to lead you to repentance." The psalmist states,

> The LORD is merciful and gracious, slow to anger and abounding in steadfast love. He will not always chide, nor will he keep his anger forever. He does not deal with us according to our sins, nor repay us according to our iniquities. For as high as the heavens are above the earth, so great is his steadfast love toward those who fear him; as far as the east is from the west, so far does he remove our transgressions from us. As a father shows compassion to his children, so the LORD shows compassion to those who fear him. For he knows our frame; he remembers that we are dust. (Psalm 103:8–14)

Your motivation to forgive is because God forgave you, and steadfast love is on display from a loving Father. When you love that child, show that child affection. Keep encouraging, even in your pain. It is a daily commitment, my friend!

Godly Grieve

The mind can take one on a roller coaster of emotions. Take regret of past mistakes and broken parent-child relationship. These are genuine human emotions, but they should come with teachable moments. The pain and tragedy can transform. Apostle Paul states, "As it is, I rejoice, not because you were grieved, but because you were grieved into repenting. For you felt a godly grief, so that you suffered no loss through us.

For godly grief produces a repentance that leads to salvation without regret, whereas worldly grief produces death. For see what earnestness this godly grief has produced in you, but also what eagerness to clear yourselves, what indignation, what fear, what longing, what zeal, what punishment! At every point you have proved yourselves innocent in the matter" (2 Corinthians 7:9–11). The worst of pain of a relationship is not beyond repair to all family members. There can be a harmony, and above all the family should bring God glory. We live this life with eternity in mind, and nothing is worth bitterness or grudges.

What does the Bible say about disciplining your child? "For the LORD disciplines those he loves, and he punishes each one he accepts as his child" (Hebrews 12:6). Loving parents discipline their children just like our heavenly Father does. When I was growing up, being disciplined via caning or spanking was not an issue with my parents and my generation. The consequences of wrongdoing were met with wrath and fire, and parents did what they deemed necessary to avoid us repeating the same mistake. Maybe they did not have or see other options.

According to the American Psychology Association, many studies have shown that physical punishment, including spanking, hitting, and other means of causing pain, can lead to increased aggression, antisocial behavior, physical injury, and mental health problems for children. Physical discipline is slowly declining as studies reveal lasting harm for children.

Should the opinions of others matter in how I discipline my child?

Guiding Your Child's Heart

What we become is what is more important than what we do. Living what was expected from me as a teen came with challenges. The desire to conform to my parents' will in their presence was the norm, but in their absence it was a different ball game! This can only be explained by understanding the depravity of the heart. Jeremiah 17:9 states, "The heart is deceitful above all things, and desperately sick; who can understand it?"

Only God himself can make the change in one's heart. Paul states in Philippians 2:13, "For it is God who works in you, both to will and to work for his good pleasure." It is pleasurable to God if parents and children walk in his will. It is God who gives us his will to energize us to fulfill his purpose. The ultimate goal is what Paul said in Romans 8:29, "For those whom he foreknew he also predestined to be conformed to the image of his Son."

As parents, we are frustrated and angry when we witness our children stray from the truth, causing strife and tension at home. Who is angry? Both parents and children. Two wrongs cannot make a right—this is an old saying applicable to parenting. The parents who want to pass the baton of faith to their children need to be intentional in the children's younger years, but it is never too late at any age to take the children's hearts, shape, and mold them! The ultimate goal is to help our children discover and ride on their own faith, not only having a change of outward behavior but also totally surrendering from within their hearts.

Boundaries

What are healthy boundaries for my children to maintain healthy relationships? In my earlier years of parenting I, found myself saying *don't* and *no* to my children. It is a work in process, but I am better. Family standards and expectations are important, with a parent-child relationship that allows for free communication and expression for engagement. In the case of swaying of God's Word, this can be addressed, and if discipline is applied, then they understand *no* and *don't*.

The Plea

The following is a client's plea.

Lucy,

Yesterday I and my wife received some bad news about our daughter's struggle with substance abuse, missing work, calling in sick, lying to her boss, and now being homeless. She has relocated to another state and has blocked our phone!

Well, as a believer in the Lord Jesus Christ and a hardworking father, I am disappointed, angry, and broken. Sometimes Satan takes me on this road trip of guilt as a failed parent. What did we do wrong? Honestly, the news I received hurt my heart, and my wife shedded tears. I am broken!

However, after a deep conversation, my wife said to me, "I can either cry about this, or I can do something about it." We chose to do something about it instead.

Therefore, our pity party lasted less than fifteen minutes, and twenty minutes later, we had a better solution to this issue. We called a trusted friend, who referred us to a biblical counselor at their local church. The counselor suggested we have our daughter evaluated for mental illness and get to the root cause of her alcoholism and substance abuse. Yes, I understand I need to pray, but I can't. We cannot get hold of our daughter. Hopefully she can listen to her grandmother, whom she seems to have a better relationship with, and hopefully she seeks help.

There are no perfect words to a hurting friend or parent in pain, but giving practical advice along with prayers is helpful. Prayer is great, a first line of defense accompanied with referral or sometimes radical decisions, such as calling emergency numbers in case one is suicidal. It is important to understand science is the work of God, and if it is well integrated with the truth of the Word of God, it works wonders. I speak from my personal experience and the testimonies of many. Are there conspiracy theories? Absolutely, but discernment is a virtue in this fallen world.

When you get blindsided by things beyond your control, ask yourself, "What am I going to do today to get me out of this challenge?"

A common phrase is "It's okay to say you are not okay." Admitting vulnerability to a trusted friend, family member, or a professional is advised. There is another common phrase: "A problem shared is half solved." This is a mental help in times of challenge.

Routine helps me have optimism and peace in my life. In the quiet hours of the morning, jump-starting the day with the Lord regardless of what happens. Do your best to choose peace over pity.

Everyday Tool of Steadfast Love Till Eternity

This book has been an elaborate discussion of one thing: God is the only one who makes sense in your parenting journey, reflecting the biblical truth that faithful obedience, character formation, and discipleship in the hearts of our children will not be the result of fear. "There is no fear in love. But perfect love drives out fear because fear has to do with punishment. The one who fears is not made perfect in love. We love because he first loved us" (1 John 4:18–19). "But rather deep security in the fact that they are relentlessly loved; Follow God's example, therefore, as dearly loved children and walk in the way of love, just as Christ loved us and gave himself up for us as a fragrant offering and sacrifice to God" (Ephesians 5:1–2).

My family visits to my grandmother's house over the

Christmas holidays never ceased to amaze me, I listened with amusement to a mother (sixty-four years) and son (forty years) talk. I remember vividly the conversation.

> **Grandma**: Watani Wakwa (my son).
>
> **Dad**: Maitu (Mother), why don't you agree with my plans for the farm?
>
> **Grandma**: I respect your age and your accomplishments, but you will always be my child to me first! Listen to me—my word is final!
>
> **Dad**: Noguo Maitu (Yes, ma'am).

My no-nonsense grandma was loaded with wisdom and nonnegotiable talks for that generation!

Parenting never stops, no matter the age. Your children need your guidance and direction. Challenge them when necessary and cheer them as they gain their wings to soar. Don't we learn from them too? Absolutely, we teach and learn from them!

How about the monologue? That can backfire badly!

God's Glory Revealed In Detours

Did the detours or the distracted lives of Kinto, Gina, and Tune have a reason or lesson? Joseph would be the best person to answer, and he is the epitome of how to handle suffering. "As for you, you meant evil against me, but God meant it for good, to bring it about that many people should be kept alive, as they are today" (Genesis 50:20).

As painful as they are, detours reveal God's glory, which is seen in his attributes and which end up working for your good as a parent. My parental pain and moments of suffering have revealed God's ultimate purpose for my life. Die to self and live for Christ!

Generational Gap

Parents, are you ready to bridge the generation gap? Gen Z is tech savvy. Our digital children are in dire need for human connection. A time for dialogue is a golden opportunity to build trust, or they will hide in the tech swagger.

The old saying of "Children are to be seen and not heard" is extinct. Instead, there is never a dull moment from basking in the truth, as Paul states in Ephesians 6:4, "Fathers, do not provoke your children to anger, but bring them up in the discipline and instruction of the Lord."

God Ultimately Makes Sense

The young teens who race through your house today, and the young adults who come and go on holidays, will grow up and head to their own homes one day. "Blessed is the one who perseveres under trial because, having stood the test, that person will receive the crown of life that the Lord has promised to those who love him" (James 1:12). Your faithfulness in God is your success in parenting. His grace will rescue your child to God-centered, fruitful lives.

You are blessed with the gift of children, and you need grace to carry you through this journey of imperfections. Your calling and witness has much less to do with you and me and more to do with a perfect God.

Parenting is not for the faint of heart. It is a great calling, and our God does impart with a childlike faith, as written in the gospel of Matthew: "And calling to him a child, he put him in the midst of them and said, 'Truly, I say to you, unless you turn and become like children, you will never enter the kingdom of heaven. Whoever humbles himself like this child is the greatest in the kingdom of heaven'" (Matthew 18:2–4). If you expect to be a perfect parent and have a perfect child, that is not even what God himself expects. God is patient with the process, so why can't you be? There is no better way to beat the blues than to praise God and change your parental focus to him. Praise and worship are my secret weapons.

As I write this book, the pandemic puts a thought in my head. "Do you know whom you are dealing with?" I was not surprised to see birds come to the bird feeder every morning to eat and sing. Don't the birds wake up singing? "Look at the birds of the air: they neither sow nor reap nor gather into barns, and yet your heavenly Father feeds them. Are you not of more value than they?" (Matthew 6:26).

My friend, as you worry, seek your Father, your Master. Do not divide you loyalty. Apostle Paul states, "Indeed, we felt that we had received the sentence of death. But that was to make us rely not on ourselves but on God who raises the dead" (2 Corinthians 1:9).

At any time, I enjoy the lyrics to songs, whether I'm in the kitchen, behind the wheel, or at my desk. Songs lift the burden of worry. Take Jay Stocker and his song "Faith."

> It seems like there so much to hope for
> So many dreams I wish they all could come true
> It gives me so much faith in all that you do
> Faith to see beyond what I can't see
> Faith to know that You will do great things
> I will trust You Lord, I'll always believe
> As I hold on to my faith
> Jesus you are holding on to me

Consider childlike faith, as in the example of Jesus, where he teaches that the kingdom of heaven belongs to little children!

Let us hold fast to the confession of our hope without wavering, for he who promised is faithful. As Paul would say,

"Let us hold fast the confession of our hope without wavering, for he who promised is faithful" (Hebrews 10:23).

God is able to move your children's detours to destiny as you establish growth in Christ from the reading of this book and as you strive to become this truth in your daily parenting journey. As someone once said, perfectionism is not the gift of the spirit, but joy is.

Enjoy your imperfect parenting journey with a perfect God and bring him glory! May your everyday parenting be filled with the fragrance of the most powerful force in the universe: steadfast love.

12

Beyond The Detour

> If you are ignorant of God's Word, you will always be ignorant of God's will.
> —Billy Graham

My grandmother entered eternal rest in September 2020, as I wrote this book. She lived in the twentieth and twenty-first centuries and would fondly say in Kikuyu, my mother tongue, "*Yumaga muichi na murogi na murathime.*" That translates to, "A woman's womb carries many children with variety and diversity of children who can either be a blessing or cause pain: a thief, a witch and or blessed." She knew the power of words. It is better to speak of the power of the tongue, according to proverbs. Proverbs 18:21 says, "Death and life are in the power of the tongue, and those who love it will eat its fruit." We shall unpack and discover the power in our word as parents. With nine children, my grandma had firsthand parenting in tears and in joy.

Remember our earlier discussion on the consequences of sin.

Satan is a schemer and a trickster, and he comes like an angel of light. "And no wonder, for Satan himself disguises as an angel of light. So it is not surprise, if his servants also disguises themselves as servants of righteousness. Their end will correspond their deeds" (2 Corinthians 11:14–15). The only power Satan has over our children is the power we give him. What are you declaring or saying over that child?

When I read and meditated on the verse that states, "He is ever lending generously, and his children become a blessing" (Psalm 37:26), I cannot not help but be grateful for the gift of faithful and robust children—and better still, the gift of motherhood. I know that one of my primary purposes in life is to raise God-fearing children, no matter the bumpy journey with detours. "Blessed is the man who fears the LORD, who greatly delights in his commandments! His offspring will be mighty in the land; the generation of the upright will be blessed. Wealth and riches are in his house" (Psalm 112:1–3).

God promises to answer your prayers. Isaiah 55:10–11 says, "As the rain cometh down, and the snow from heaven ... So shall my word be that goeth forth out of my mouth: it shall not return unto me void." The word *void* means empty. The remainder of verse 11 explains what it means to "not return void," saying that God's Word "will accomplish what I desire and achieve the purpose for which I sent it."

There is no better time than during the turbulent season for parents to say your faith-filled prayers and declarations over your children, overcoming Satan's fear-filled death predictions, alcohol use, drug addictions, teen pregnancies, sexual abuse, mental illness, suicide, and depression.

We will not live in or perpetuate fear but will fight with the word of truth. Nothing—no temptation, no habit—is more significant than our God!

I recently met an amazing sister in the Lord at a ladies Bible study at my church. Barbara has a zeal for the Lord and a heart for prayers in our interactions. In reading her book on prayer, *The Ultimate Prayer Guide,* she highlights, "It is not during our highly emotional events the 'wow factor' that we grow the most spiritually but in our day-by-day life experiences both pleasant and unpleasant. Faith is like a muscle that takes time to build" (Barbara Ho, *Ultimate Connection*, 2011).

Parents, in the same way as in your pain, your experiences of your journey draw you close to God and grow your faith!

As stated earlier, you must allow His will, not your will or alternative benefit—which get in the way of answered prayers—or else you will miss the blessing in the Detour.

Deeper Needs For Well-rounded Chidren

Most parents desire the blessings of the Lord, but only a few are willing to pay the price. Here is the secret to prayers, His Word and a strong family system. Let the Word of the Lord be part of your family life to nourish spiritual growth and do whatever it says. Then you will be prosperous in all you do. God spoke into being everything we see around. He said, "Let there be." Therefore when you do the same, talk life into your child's situation, declare His Word, and continue in obedience with practical wisdom and practical ideas.Establish a strong family system for spiritually fruitful,capable and well-rounded children with a healthy self-esteem and ultimate identity in Christ!

But beyond the detours of our children, we need to see their deeper needs met, the emotional and physical needs. Jesus said in John 20:21, "As the Father has sent me, even so I am sending you. And when he had said this, he breathed on them and said to them, 'Receive the Holy Spirit!'" Parents, go after your children, as God searched for Adam and Jesus for us. The Holy Spirit makes it all possible; he is a dear helper, guide, and comforter.

Prayers to guide and equip you in the parental battle and guard your child's heart.

Some parts are crafted from *God's Word* by Brooke McGlothlin, author of *Praying for Boys and Daughters: Asking God for the Things They Need Most*.

1. Lord, give my child a deep desire to listen to you, and pray often. "And he said, 'No; but I am the commander of the army of the LORD. Now I have come.' And Joshua fell on his face to the earth and worshiped and said to him, 'What does my lord say to his servant?'" (Joshua 5:14b).
2. Let my children learn early in life that to obey you, God, is the best way to the life their hearts' desires. "And Samuel said, Has the LORD as great delight in burnt offerings and sacrifices, as in obeying the voice of the LORD? Behold, to obey is better than sacrifice, and to listen than the fat of rams" (1 Samuel 15:22).
3. Lord, may my children find comfort in your ability. Lord, reach them, hold them, and rescue them. "He sent from on high, he took me; he drew me out of many waters. He rescued me from my strong enemy, from those who hated me for they were too mighty for me" (2 Samuel 22:17–18).
4. Father, Lord, may my child please you by desiring, asking for, and having a discerning heart full of wisdom. "'Give your servant therefore an understanding mind to govern your people, that I may discern between good and evil, for who is able to govern this your great people?' It pleased the Lord that Solomon had asked this. And God said to him, 'Because you have asked this, and have not asked for yourself long life or riches or the life of your enemies, but have asked for yourself understanding to discern what is right, behold, I now do according to your word. Behold, I give you a wise and discerning mind, so that none like you has been before you and none like you shall arise after you'" (1 Kings 3:9–12).

5. Lord, let my child find confidence in you in good and hard times. If he doesn't know what to do, let him keep his eyes fixed on you. "O our God, will you not execute judgment on them? For we are powerless against this great horde that is coming against us. We do not know what to do, but our eyes are on you" (2 Chronicles 20:12).
6. Lord, give my child a great desire to accept your Word, and store up your commands within her so her ears will turn to your wisdom. "My son, if you receive my words and treasure up my commandments with you, making your ear attentive to wisdom and inclining your heart to understanding" (Proverbs 2:1–2).
7. May my child keep under your control by the power of the Holy Spirit and not give in to anger, people, and situations. "A fool gives full vent to his spirit, but a wise man quietly holds it back" (Proverbs 29:11).
8. Lord, give my child the ability to rise above the traps of people pleasing, and let my child learn to trust you and rely on you. "The fear of man lays a snare, but whoever trusts in the LORD is safe" (Proverbs 29:25).
9. Lord, may my children walk in the security of your assigned worth to them. Instill in them a strong work ethic and good health to accomplish tasks. Give my children a heart that desires to extend their works to the very noble among us. "Let the thief no longer steal, but rather let him labor, doing honest work with his own hands, so that he may have something to share with anyone in need" (Ephesians 4:28).
10. Lord, protect my child for the right spouse, with respect and Godly honor. For my daughter, let her be a woman of joy and laughter whose Christ-centered character is what makes her most beautiful. (Proverbs 31:10).
11. And every time you hear Jesus, whisper, "Follow me" (Matthew 4:19), my child will do so with great grace.

12. Lord, create in my children clean hearts, and renew a right spirit within them. "Create in me a clean heart, O God, and renew a right spirit within me" (Psalm 51:10).
13. May my child walk after you, God, his Father. May he fear you and obey your voice, and may he hide your Word in his heart that he may not sin against you. "I have stored up your word in my heart, that I might not sin against you" (Psalm 119:11).
14. May my child serve you and hold fast to you. "You shall walk after the LORD your God and fear him and keep his commandments and obey his voice, and you shall serve him and hold fast to him" (Deuteronomy 13:4).
15. Dear Lord, help my child to be strong and courageous and not fear. "Be strong and courageous. Do not fear or be in dread of them, for it is the LORD your God who goes with you. He will not leave you or forsake you" (Deuteronomy 31:6).
16. Like Timothy, Lord, help my child walk before you, as King David walked, with integrity of heart and uprightness, doing according to all that you have commanded him and keeping your statutes and rules. "And as for you, if you will walk before me, as David your father walked, with integrity of heart and uprightness, doing according to all that I have commanded you, and keeping my statutes and my rules" (1 Kings 9:4).
17. Lord, may my child be an example to believers in speech, in conduct, in love, in faith, and in purity. "Let no one despise you for your youth, but set the believers an example in speech, in conduct, in love, in faith, in purity" (1 Timothy 4:12).
18. May my child honor his father and mother. "'Honor your father and mother' (this is the first commandment with a promise)" (Ephesians 6:2).
19. May my child have love that issues from a pure heart and a good conscience and a sincere faith. "The aim of

our charge is love that issues from a pure heart and a good conscience and a sincere faith" (1 Timothy 1:5).
20. May my child think on whatever is true, whatever is honorable, whatever is just, whatever is pure, whatever is commendable. If there is any excellence, if there is anything worthy of praise, may he think about these things. "Finally, brothers, whatever is true, whatever is honorable, whatever is just, whatever is pure, whatever is lovely, whatever is commendable, if there is any excellence, if there is anything worthy of praise, think about these things" (Philippians 4:8).

Prayer for a Parent in the Crucible

My prayer to you in the crucible is to let God use the messiness of your parenting to make you and your child more like him and know you are born to a living hope, as Apostle Peter states:

> Blessed be the God and Father of our Lord Jesus Christ! According to his great mercy, he has caused us to be born again to a living hope through the resurrection of Jesus Christ from the dead, to an inheritance that is imperishable, undefiled, and unfading, kept in heaven for you, who by God's power are being guarded through faith for a salvation ready to be revealed in the last time. In this you rejoice, though now for a little while, if necessary, you have been grieved by various trials, so that the tested genuineness of your faith—more precious than gold that perishes though it is tested by fire—may be found to result in praise and glory and honor at the revelation of Jesus Christ. Though you have not seen him, you love him. Though you do not now see him, you believe in him and rejoice with joy that is

inexpressible and filled with glory, obtaining the outcome of your faith, the salvation of your souls. (1 Peter1:3–9)

What a fitting way to end our reading: with an assurance of a living hope in your parental journey!

Where Do You Go from Here? Go Deeper in Your Parenting Journey

Now that you have read through this book, my prayer to you is to show steadfast love to your children with a loving God who listens and makes sense in the storm and detours. May you find strength in the face of pain and hard realities of your parental journey.

Video Series Studies: Introduction

Following are some of the topic to the upcoming video series, to encourage you to reinforce your reading through small groups or Bible study. Pray and talk, share these concepts, practical wisdom and practical ideas and help other parents develop a great parent mindset.

Practical tips and Content based on biblical perspective:

- Seasons of Parenting;the "mom code"
- Understanding detours and strongholds :Sad reality of addiction,Choosing recovery
- The model parent :Standing out in Fit -In Generation,
- Grace based parenting
- Unconditinal love,Tough Love, Choices and freedom
- Navigate social media challenges, cyberbullying, identity, peer preesure
- Communication and Healthy conflict resolutions

- Hard realities talk on:dating violence,What the culture is not telling you about sex
- The Heart of your child and mental illness: depression, self injury, suicide
- Pray For Me I am A parent:Power Of Prayer and Living side by side

Session 1: Seasons When Nothing Makes Sense (Gospel Parenting Worldview, Seasons in Parenting When God Does Not Make Sense, but He Does!)

Session 2: The Storm Barrier; Detour (Parenting a Call to Live in the Light of Grace and Hope of Jesus Christ)

Session 3: God Makes Sense(The Attributes Of God)

Session 4: (Parenting the Privilege of Being an Ambassador of Jesus Christ to Your Child

Session 5: Grace Abounds (Carrying the Burden of Parenting with God's Grace: What Does the Gospel Say about God, You as a Parent, Your Word, and Your Child? Grace to the Afflicted)

Session 6: GPS signal lost;navigation rerouting (Exhausted Parent: Big Picture Worldview Parenting to Navigate through God's Call and Be Joyful

Session7:From Faith To Faith—Parent in Pain(Journey of Faith from beginning and to every nitty gritty details)

Session 8: We Do Not Know What to Do, but Our Eyes Are on You (Despair}

Session 9: Pray For Me, I am A Parent

Session10: The DNA of God's Steadfast Love (Parenting Far Beyond Behavior, Understanding Your Child's Heart and the Gospel; Grace-Based Parenting)

Session 11: Perfectly Imperfect (Everyday Parenting through the Lens of Christ, Deepening Your Relationship with God, Imperfect Parent)

Session 12: Beyond The Detours

Bibliographical References

Dobson, James. *When God Doesn't Make Sense*. Tyndale House, *1993*.

Evans, Tony. *Detours*. B&H, *2017*.

Kimmel, Tim. *Grace Based Parenting*. Family Matters, *2010*.

Terkeurst, Lysa. *It's Not Ssupposed to Be This Way*. Thomas Nelson, *2018*.

Tripp, David Paul. *Parenting*. Crossway, 2016.

About the Author

Lucy Wanjiru Watani-Simiyu was born in Kenya. She and her family migrated to America from Kenya, Africa, and God has faithfully established her family. She resides in Houston, Texas, with her husband of twenty-eight years, Bob Simiyu, and they are blessed with three sons: Kevin, Derrick, and Roy and one teenage daughter Angel.

Drawing on her long experience as a mother, teacher, biblical counselor, crisis care hospice nurse, and public health professional, she brings hope to parents in pain who are have almost given up on their role of parenting due to their children's detours or delayed spiritual maturation and consequently are in doubt of their parenting abilities. She draws from her training as a biblical counselor from the College of Biblical Studies, Houston. She has continued to serve in her local church, Bear Creek Baptist Church, in Katy, Texas, for over a decade as a connector (biblical counselor). Lucy is a mental health advocate and coach from American Association of Christian Counsellors(AACC), volunteer for Mental Health Start Removing Stigma Association (MH STARS), and she is currently involved in creating mental health awareness in collaboration with mental health coaches and volunteers, reaching out to thousands of people regarding mental issues, suicidal teens and adults, at-risk teens, and all others who need God's hope, love, Word, and prayers.

Lucy is an experienced health care and human services consultant, a nurse, and a public health professional. She has several years of service in the United States. She has extensive experience in management and provision of clinical services. Lucy is a capacity builder for health care professionals and previously served as an educator in developing countries, mainly in Sub-Saharan Africa. Lucy has also worked in a variety of hospice settings as a crisis care nurse, educating and counseling families to cope with end-of-life issues and subsequent transitions. She is a graduate of National University with a master's in public health, specializing in health promotion. She studied global health management at Osnabruck University, Germany. Lucy is also a graduate of the College of Biblical Studies, Houston, with a BSc in Christian counseling. Lucy is a licensed vocational nurse. Lucy wears many hats and integrates her passion for service with her formal training as a teacher, nurse, Biblical counselor and public health professional. She has a passion for and commitment to health promotion, specifically families, geriatrics and adolescent health issues, with an emphasis on the healing power of faith in God.